# PRACTICAL PROJECT MANAGEMENT

W J Taylor &
T F Watling

# PRACTICAL
# PROJECT
# MANAGEMENT

 BUSINESS BOOKS—*LONDON*

First published in Britain in 1973

© William John Taylor and Thomas Francis Watling, 1973

ISBN 0 220 66237 1

This book has been set in 10 on 12 point Times Roman and
photoset and printed in Malta by St Paul's Press Ltd,
for the publisher, Business Books Limited
Registered office: 110 Fleet Street, London EC4A 2JL
Publishing office: Mercury House, Waterloo Road, London SE1 8UL

# Contents

**Part Two   PEOPLE AND PROJECTS**

**Part Three   PROJECT PLANNING AND PROGRESSING**

# Illustrations

# Acknowledgements

The authors thank ICL for allowing them to have the book published. They thank Mr A McG Leckie for reading the book in manuscript and for his helpful comments. They also thank Miss Gloria Williams and Miss Jocelyn Patey for typing the manuscript.

*W J Taylor, T F Watling*

# Part One

# PROJECT MANAGEMENT APPROACH

# 1

# Projects and Project Management

A project may be defined as a group of connected activities with a defined starting point, a defined finish and need for central intelligence to direct it. Project management has only become a recognised form of management during the past half century or so, yet in reality projects have been subject to management for centuries. The ancient Egyptians may not have called the man in charge of constructing a pyramid a project manager yet that is what he was.

The famous engineers of the nineteenth century were often in effect project managers. Isambard Kingdom Brunel may have been appointed The Engineer of the Great Western Railway, but he was effectively the project manager responsible for the planning and construction of the line from Bristol, Temple Meads, to London, Paddington. He did not have the benefit of modern project management techniques, such as PERT or DCF. Nonetheless, his was in essence a project management approach. One central intelligence looked at the Great Western Railway as a whole and drove the project forward, overcoming the mass of technical and managerial problems. Fairly typically for a project manager, he also had his fair share of political problems. Factions among the ownership of the company tried to have his technical and management decisions reversed. He had to attend meetings of parliamentary committees as well as public meetings to fight for his project. He knew and understood the problems of project survival—a subject of considerable importance to some modern project managers.

I K Brunel was responsible for many projects. During the Crimean War, like many others, he was scandalised by the state of Scutari Hospital, disclosed by Florence Nightingale. He was invited by the Permanent Secretary at the War Office to design an improved hospital to be prefabricated in England and erected in the Crimea. He became involved in a dispute with War Office Contracts Department over his initiative in placing a contract for buildings for a hospital of 1000 beds before any form of authority had been given. His reply to their complaints gives some indication of what project management is about. He wrote:

> Such a course may possibly be unusual in the execution of government work, but it only involves an amount of responsibility which men in my profession are accustomed to take.... It is only by the prompt and independent actions of a single individual entrusted with such powers that expedition can be secured and vexations and mischievous delays avoided.... These buildings if wanted at all, must be wanted before they can possibly arrive.

He emphasised two points: first the need for a single individual looking at a project as a whole; second the perrenial problem of all project managers—timescales are always tight.

## 1:1  PROJECT DEFINITIONS

Are there such things as typical projects? In truth there cannot be but all projects have life cycles which in terms of project management typify the management responses needed to manage them. Probably the first sort of project tasks that spring to mind as typical are in the field of civil engineering construction; bridges, dams, motorways, new airfields or docks. In all of these there is a clear initial project or construction phase, followed by a phase of use, during which they have merely to be maintained in use. In advanced technology "typical" examples are in the development of a new aircraft or computer.

In the field in which we work there is the development and bringing into operation of new computer systems. The creation of a new power station or oil refinery is a project. In yet another field the construction and setting up of a new motel is a project. The project starts with the decision to open a new hotel say at Norwich. It ends when the hotel manager and his staff finally sign off the project as complete and start providing a hotel service to their customers. During the project stage there will be many parties involved in the work: acquiring the land, drawing up plans, negotiating permissions, building the hotel, furnishing and equipping it, laying out the grounds and sign-posting them. Many thousands of activities will be involved and many dozens of contracting and supplying firms may be involved. However, once the hotel is up and running the emphasis changes to one of steady running and routine and efficient customer service of a very high standard over a comparatively limited range of items.

Altogether different projects but which still demand the same sort of planning and execution are those that have to do with disaster relief in order to get a damaged area back to normal. Explorations, endurance sailing voyages and space travel are all projects. They all involve the bringing together of many kinds of resources, detailed planning towards an end event and a project implementation. The launch of a new institute such as a university or technical college lends itself to project management, even if the academic mind shys away from the idea. The opening of a new radio station, the launch of a new pop group, the opening of a new branch of a bank or a retail chain may sensibly be treated as a project. If some new activity is complete in itself, has a clear start and finish point and an examination of its complexities, risks and uncertainties suggests that a central intelligence is needed to guide it to a successful conclusion then a project management approach should be considered.

## 1:2  PROJECT STAGES

Broadly speaking the majority of projects deal with the construction or establishment stage of an undertaking. The project stage is followed by a running or care and maintenance stage. The division between these two stages is not always clearly defined. Nonetheless the two phases are distinct and require a very different approach. The man who is a first-class hotel manager probably will not be the right man to establish a new hotel on a green field site. If you look more closely at the stages that really constitute a project you will find more than the two stages mentioned above. An examination of these stages also gives many clues as to why a more centralised approach is really necessary. Whatever names are chosen for the stages, and there are many because of the many varieties of projects, there are four or five time-phased sets of activity areas in a project.

*Concept stage.*  This is when the basic objectives of the project are formulated. It may be that a need has been clearly identified which the project is, hopefully, going to satisfy. It may be that an idea has been created which seems worth pursuing. In the everyday world a company may have seen a need for a new type of four-wheeled bicycle and start to formulate a concept for it. In the military world someone may have had the idea for a series of orbiting bombs and a concept is formulated for this. The concept stage does not stop at just saying: "We are going to have an orbiting bomb." It goes on to say roughly how big it will be, at what height it should orbit and what type of guidance system it ought to have. The concept stage deals with basic requirements defined sufficiently to enable the idea to be fully recognised. In project management one often talks of baselines. This simply means a platform of planning and knowledge at any one time from which one can chart future activities. There is a baseline derived from the concept stage which may go under various names but which we will call the "project aim."

The project aim includes the following fundamental statements:

1     A description of the basic requirements of the project in the detail at that time required and possible—for example, the housing estate will be about 500 houses ranging from 15% three-bedroomed terraced houses to 10% five-bedroomed detached and suitable mixture of other houses

2     The general technical approach—for example, the houses will be aluminium throughout and use a central estate heating plan

3     From this technical approach statement can come the general ideas on the technological problems if any

4     Estimates of costs, timescales, prices, resources, planning procedures, capital, specialists, etc

5     Identification of any other relevant facts, support activities or facilities that may be required

The project aim will be meaningful in that a project choice can be made from it—that is, proceed, abandon or change.

*Project definition.* This is the second baseline and it is during the definition stage that the items comprising the concept would be translated to more definitive data such as performance specifications. The plans would be more detailed and schedules of the work broadly defined. The culmination would be a complete specification of the project so that no doubt existed as to the size, shape, performance, reliability, etc, requirements with an updated version of all the items previously mentioned under the project aim. There is again an opportunity to abandon the project if some aspect is now found to be outside the allowable continuation criteria.

Once a project definition has been completed the third and fourth stages may vary with the type of project. For example, in an engineering project involving the creation of, say, a new printing machine it is likely that the third stage will be in two parts. The first part will be concerned with designing and engineering the new machine up to the building of a prototype model. When the prototype is proved one can claim to have a viable product as far as design is concerned. One can move on to production, which is the second part of this third stage. Whether in the end these things are called parts or stages does not really matter, it is the distinction that is important.

In the case of a new housing estate the design and development will be the preparation of working documents. Production will be the construction of the estate. There is unlikely to be a prototype. In essence, however, the two parts still exist.

*Design and development stage.* This is the third identifiable stage whether or not a prototype is involved and whatever one decide to call the parts. In some projects considerable research and development may be required to conclude this stage satisfactorily. Where a prototype is involved one must ensure that:

1   The prototype performs the functions specified at the project definition stage
2   All changes, additions and modifications that were approved have been incorporated in the prototype
3   The drawings and data from which the production can commence agree with the prototype and are complete and accurate

*Production stage.* In this stage one has to make sure that anything one is making or supplying conforms to the data previously established. This means that:

1   All items have to be tested, if this is appropriate, or at least inspected
2   No change to the original data must be allowed without reference to some change authority

*Operational stage.* The project is now in operation and has been handed over to the customer or user. Changes to the project have to be authorised and maintenance may be involved.

The brief outline of project stages above have analogies in all forms of different projects. It is advantageous to identify them whatever the project so that it can proceed in an organised and effective manner.

## 1:3   RESEARCH AND DEVELOPMENT

This is in one sense a special case for projects. It is quite common in companies that do not have the kind of implementation projects mentioned above to have engineering or research and development projects, and recognised as such, even though their value is small in financial terms. There can be just as many disasters in these small projects as there are in larger ones if they are not run properly. They are often risky. They will have to have the same tight controls over finance and value if they are to survive like their bigger brothers. Often the "customer" in these cases is the marketing organisation of the same company. Because the project is small there would seem to be no incentive to employ a project manager as such and the engineer in charge assumes the role if not the title.

Because by their very nature research and development projects are invariably the start of something else—a new process, a new product or a service—the total cost of everything which rests on the project should be considered before deciding that an R & D project is too small to run properly as a project. Many of these projects lead on to development, engineering, manufacture and sale of a product. These later stages may involve many times the expenditure of the initial development project. Delays and overrun costs on the development project may be magnified many times in their effect on the later *program*.

There is, unfortunately, plenty of evidence of the type of activity shown in Figure 1.1.

The safest and most economic method overall is to adopt the practice as illustrated in Figure 1.2. Figures 1.1 and 1.2 are applicable to all projects not just R & D type work.

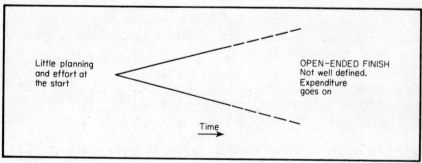

**Figure I.I** PROJECT ACTIVITY, OPEN-ENDED

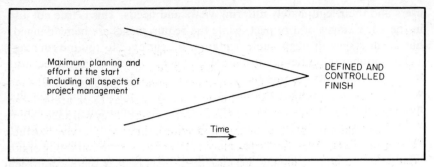

**Figure I.2  PROJECT ACTIVITY, DEFINED FINISH**

## 1:4  NEED FOR PROJECT MANAGEMENT

The need for project mangement arises from the complexity, risk and uncertainty involved in an undertaking rather than from its mere size. Size is sometimes used as a criterion of the need for project management, but this is because in practice the larger the undertaking in a given field, the greater the complexity, risk and uncertainty.

## 1:5  COMPLEXITY

Complexity of the undertaking is the first and most important criterion of the need for project management. The prime cause of complexity is the number of different parties involved in the project. At one end lie the users or potential users of a completed project. Where a power station may provide power for a million homes and factories, the number of users for project purposes is not a million users unless the project embraces the wiring of the million outlets. In practise the power station has a single user in most countries: the national or distributive grid takes the total output of the power station.

For many projects, however, there is more than one user, who has a say in the design and running of a project. For instance, in a projected scheme for automating the accounting of the London Stock Exchange over 300 firms of stockbrokers and jobbers had a say in agreeing the user requirements. In the case of the highly successful London Airport Cargo EDP Scheme some eighteen international airlines and 150 freight forwarding agents as well as HM Customs and Excise had a say in agreeing the requirements. Some mechanism is needed for reconciling such a large number of users and their legitimately differing views and needs. This is true not just in the early stages of a project, while the requirements are being defined, but at all stages through implementation till cut over to routine running.

The number of parties involved in the implementation of the project also involves complexity. Within the organisation responsible for the project—whether it is a national corporation or private company—the larger the number of departments involved the greater the complexity. The actual work may be done entirely by one company or organisation. This is, however, unusual on large projects. There may be several contracting firms involved. Indeed on construction projects for power stations, oil refineries or smelters, there may be literally hundreds of subcontracting firms involved.

The greater the number of parties involved the greater the complexity of the project and the greater the need for a central project management. Later in this book, we shall be expanding on the great importance of a well-defined set of project requirements and the imperative need to control changes to those requirements. The larger the number of parties involved the more difficult it is to see what the effect of change will be and to ensure that each party affected by a change is consulted before the change in requirement is accepted. Within a single organisation it may be relatively easy to adjust schedules to compensate for delays and changes. However, when dozens or hundreds of separate firms are involved considerably greater effort and negotiation is necessary to make the required schedule adjustments. Similarly the task of trading-off time, cost and performance is made very much more difficult as the number of parties increases. To the layman it may look as though a tractor controls itself, it is only when he tries to drive one himself that he appreciates the skill required. It may seem as though a project involving a dozen different parties will run itself. It won't. The greater the number of parties, the greater the complexity and need for central project control.

Another factor involving complexity is geographical spread. Are the people involved in the project located in different places or even different countries or continents? We have worked in companies where communication between managers on the same site but on different sides of the main road proved very difficult. Even in these days of good telecommunications, there is no real substitute for the face-to-face meeting to reconcile contentious views. An additional geographical factor of complexity comes when the preparatory work is done remotely from the operational site. The complexity increases if equipment developed in different factories has to be brought together for testing, either on site or at one of the factories. If equipment has to be moved across national frontiers in the course of the project this can add to complexity.

Yet another factor making for complexity or otherwise is the competence and experience of the end user of the project, whether that end user belongs to the organisation running the project or whether he is an outside user or customer. In any field, the inexperienced user can be a trial. He needs more mothering than an experienced user. Everything has to be explained more carefully. The inexperienced user often finds it difficult to appreciate just how important it is to know what he is doing when he finally approves the user requirements specification. In particular he does not appreciate the havoc caused by late changes to the specification.

1:6   RISK

Complexity and risk tend to go hand in hand. There may be very real practical difficulties, which have to be overcome if a project is to be successful. These may range from "simple" practical problems such as a computer being delivered into a building to which there is no easy access, or heavy generating plant of a size and weight which the law will not normally allow to be carried on public roads. The problems may effectively relate to the field of technology in which the project lies. There may be a need to develop something larger, faster or harder than has been produced before. The need to develop carbon fibre for the Rolls-Royce RB211 project is an instance of how the need for development work increased the complexity of a project. However, it is not just great technological advances that lead to complexity or risk in a project. Almost any part of a project, which involves a "first" or something new, adds to the risk and complexity of a project and hence to the need for firm project management.

The whole question of financial risk will of course be taken into account in the initial evaluation of any project. For instance, the profitability of a new copper mining project obviously depends on the price at which copper can be sold when the mine is producing. This does not of itself increase the need for project management. However, there are certain financial risks that do increase that need. Any project of a development nature carries the seed of costs which, like Jack's beanstalk, grow beyond all reason. In almost any project delay may give rise to increased cost. An initial evaluation of these financial risks helps in making the decision on whether a project manager is needed. What are the consequences of failure to meet dates, performance or cost? If the project is being undertaken for a customer, what is the value of that customer's business and goodwill? What is the risk to your firm of losing them? The extent to which the risks in a project fall to any particular party frequently depend upon the tightness with which the contracts are written. As between the parties involved, whoever shoulders systems responsibility normally find themselves with the major risk.

Complexity, newness, risk and uncertainty all go together and call for project management. Size of itself does not require project management, but size tends to go with the factors we have enumerated.

## 1:7  SUMMARY—SIMPLE CONCEPT

If we strip away from project management the "buzz" words that so often accompany it we are left with a simple concept: a central technical and management interface for a particular project looking outwards from the company it represents to the customer or user the company must satisfy. This central interface must, by the same token, look across all internal company resources involved in the task with any subcontractors involved, and ensure that the project is effectively carried out.

Management itself, paradoxically often does not acknowledge that project management should exist yet has no difficulty in agreeing that a company must be managed. Project management is a part of management—it is not wholly conventional in that its authority arises out of the project and its needs; it tends to emphasise planning and control perhaps more than a line operating department; it accentuated leadership and team working; it lays great stress on user satisfaction through agreed performance criteria and achievement.

Another aspect, about which more will be written later, is the accountability one can obtain when one sets up a project properly. All at once one has a peg on which to hang the technical, managerial, administrative, personnel and accounting functions and responsibilities for perhaps a significant part of a company's business. Without such a set up one would be likely to stop short at the boundaries of the functional line divisions of the company. In a project one must go beyond these boundaries because there is work and danger to be covered beyond them. Some companies tend to do it halfheartedly through their salesmen; others through various committees and other devices. We want to show that a project deserves more, that the company or supplier can achieve more and that the customer will be better satisfied by the use of project management to the full.

# 2

# Benefits and Costs
# of Project Management

There are considerable benefits to be derived from project management. Unfortunately it is not always obvious to senior management, when they start a project, that the project will benefit from project management. At that stage the costs that will be incurred by adopting a project management approach are all too obvious, while the benefits seem too vague and uncertain.

We know of one case where top management saw the light quite quickly. A medium-sized firm based in the United Kingdom had about 10 000 employees and an annual turnover of about £50 million in a field of advanced technology. Turnover was concentrated on production of standard production line items and was increasing by about 20% a year. The company was effectively run by eight directors and twenty-five divisional managers. The board were keen to extend their activities. They wanted to cease being mere suppliers to the giants of the industry and become prime contractors for advanced projects. The opportunity came with a large government project, let us call it "Cox's Project." The company was determined to get the order. It quoted a low and highly competitive price. The price incidentally was calculated in a manner that made no provision for project management costs, the cost of supervising subcontracts, or the cost involved in financing subcontractors and own work in progress. The tendered price had also been rounded down to the nice whole figure of £2 million. In due course the order was received on the basis of completion with two years. The project was to satisfy certain performance criteria and was to be subject to an acceptance test at the end of the two-year period. The project was subject to a penalty clause—or more correctly a liquidated damages clause. This provided for liquidated damages of £10 000 a week to be paid to the government department for each week of delay, after the first four weeks delay. Being full of expansionist spirit at the time of the tender, the company had failed to place a top limit on the penalties.

Cox's Project was to be co-ordinated by a committee. This consisted of three directors and eight of the divisional manager sitting under the chairmanship of the assistant managing director. He had originally been concerned about the size of the committee but earlier meetings at the tender stage indicated that it was the minimum number possible. The first meeting, full of optimism was held two weeks after the order was received. When it came to fixing the next meeting, after much fingering of diaries, a date six week's ahead was fixed. Even this was only possible because the assistant managing director lent fairly heavily on his colleagues.

The second meeting was long and acrimonious. The standard product line items were coming along satisfactorily to schedule. Problems had arisen in agreeing the specifications of the development items. Two of the three subcontractors were already indicating scheduling problems. One of the divisional managers had deduced that the tender allowed no time or money for the acceptance tests, which would take at least four weeks. All three subcontractors in the negotiations for their contracts were demanding progress payments. Much of the information needed by the meeting was not available because it was not included in the relevant manager's brief.

Next day the directors concerned met to discuss what should be done about Cox's Project. The company was clearly heading for disaster. Quite apart from the probability of delays, extra costs and penalties, the project instead of acting as a loss leader to pull in future big project business was likely to draw considerable odium down on the company as well as a degree of ridicule in the trade. The finance director was particularly concerned at the idea of unlimited penalties and overrun costs.

In their discussion the directors agreed on the existance of a number of problem areas. Each one of them and each one of the divisional managers had many other duties. Important though the project was it only represented some 2% of the company's turnover in each of the two years of its life. Yet it was clear that as they were then organised they would all have to give a great deal of their time to Cox's Project. That management panacea, delegation, was suggested. However, first time round, it became clear that forty-one departmental managers were involved. To simply delegate the problem to them and leave them to get on with it would be disastrous. In the end it would result in even more of the company's management time being taken up.

It might even have taken up more of senior management time in reconciling entrenched departmental views.

Apart from the amount of senior management time and the difficulty of getting them all together at one time and place, a serious problem arose because much of the real work was done at least two levels down from the divisional managers. Some divisional managers came to the meetings fully briefed. Others were completely stumped by any question and unable to agree to any modification in their plans without referring back to their staff. Two of the divisional managers had tried to overcome this problem by coming to the second project meeting with a couple of supporting staff each. Had each principal at the meetings brought a couple of supporters the meetings would have become totally unmanageable—more like a parliament than a meeting of business managers intent on executive action.

Further problems had arisen because of the long line of communication back from the project meetings to the people who actually did the work. These were compounded by the paucity of direct contact between the people in different departments who were actually working on the project.

The final outcome of the directors' meeting was to appoint a project manager. A company announcement was published making the appointment, stating that the board regarded the successful completion of the project as of the highest priority and finally formally stating that the project manager would have the backing of the managing director and would have access to him.

This project manager inherited more than his fair share of problems but was able none the less to bring the Cox's Project to a successful conclusion. No penalties were paid and he had to call on the managing director for assistance only once.

Even quite a large and important project may only directly involve a few percentage points of the year's turnover for many departments of a large company. Nonetheless those departments may be providing a contribution to the project, which is vital both in terms of timeliness and performance. A departmental manager may well allow his contribution to the project to slip by a month in order to obtain—in departmental terms—a better utilisation of his department resources. However, if his department's contribution is on the critical path of the project, the company picture may be very different. Suppose also that the company pays 12% a year in interest charges on its overdraft. Then the cost of delay due to that departmental manager's sound planning of his own resources will be £20 000 in interest charges alone. Needless to say there will be other costs due to dislocations of the project plans and possibly because of penalties.

## 2:1   CENTRALISATION BENEFIT

One of the major benefits of appointing a project manager for a project is that one central intelligence is totally concerned about a project and committed to its success. The project manager throughout the life of the project is able to see the project as a whole and is able to see how the parts fit together and contribute to that whole. From his knowledge of the project plan—and from his network of activities—he can tell the ramifications of any delay or failure to reach the agreed performance standards. He is in a position to know when a departmental manager may be allowed some deviation from plan. He also knows which activities are of critical importance to the project and must be held to schedule almost whatever the cost may be.

## 2:2   TRADE-OFFS

This leads into the area of trade-offs. It is here that a good project manager can have a great effect on the success of his project and deliver great benefits to his company by minimising the disruption caused to the company by project problems. It is obvious to most of us that time, cost and performance are related. This is just as true of the project as a whole as it is of individual project activities. A popular question of the old-fashioned mathematics was: if it takes two men six hours to dig a ditch ten yards long, how long will it take four men to dig the same ditch? The presumed correct answer was three hours, a simple illustration of the trade-off between time and resources. In real life the relationship even in an elementary case like this, may not be so simple. On the one hand, the men may get in each other's way, may argue or waste time in conversation or playing cards; on the other hand, the old team of two may compete with the new one or refrain from taking such frequent breaks, knowing that other teams are watching them. They may even increase output because they see the arrival of the additional team of two as the first step towards their losing their jobs. Although the relationship is not as simple as it appears, this business of trade-offs is crucial to the success of any large project. The project manager, who really knows his project, knows when he can save his company money by spending an extra £10 000. He can also calculate when it is better to complete a project late rather than bring the project back on schedule.

Although some resources may be in critically short supply, it is broadly true to equate resources with cost. Let us look at the simple cost curve in Figure 2.1. This illustrates the relationship of cost and time in a simple project activity. For this particular activity there is a particular point at which cost will be at a minimum. If the number of men or machines allotted

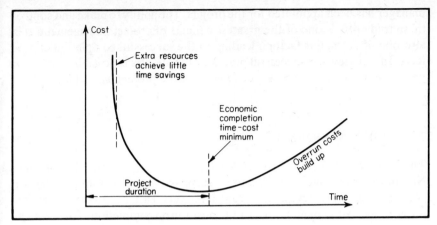

Figure 2.1 PROJECT TIME/COST CURVE

to the activity is reduced the activity will take longer to complete. Furthermore, the longer the activity takes to complete, so the cost gradually rises. This is partly because of the costs of overheads and supervision and partly because of keeping work in progress for a longer period. On the other hand, if extra resources are piled into this activity—above the optimum level—the time taken to complete the activity will be reduced. However, the time will not be reduced in proportion to the extra resources put into the activity. Economists explain this phenomenon by the "law of diminishing returns." Once more than the optimum level of resources is allotted to the activity, they require more co-ordination and they get in each other's way. There comes a point at which extra resources can be put into an activity without any reduction in completion time. There may even come a point when additional resources are counter productive and increase the time taken rather then reduce it.

When a project manager initially puts his project plan together, he will try to have each activity at the optimum resources and time point. In practice it is not a point but a range of time over which costs will be at a minimum. In practice also his first network will show the project manager that compromise is necessary and that if the project as a whole is to be executed in a certain timescale or at minimum cost it is necessary for some activities to have more money spent on them in order to reduce the time they take. This happens not only at the initial planning stage but also continuously throughout the project as progress is reviewed. In fact not only time and cost are traded against each other but also time and cost against performance. It is possible to make these trade-offs effectively only if a project manager has been appointed for the project. The ability to make and control these trade offs is one of the greatest benefits of project management. It is also one of the major factors, leading to the successful completion of projects. In our view the successful practice of trade-offs is possible only when you have one central intelligence looking at the project as a whole.


## 2:3   EARLY WARNING

The next major benefit of project management is early warning of problems. No company management likes to be surprised by news of huge delays or overrun cost. A project manager can, at the very least, keep a close watch on progress against plan and forecast the position on completion of the project. An effective project manager will not only give early warning of serious problems but will, hopefully, do something about it. In any event, the earlier the warning of trouble, the more time there is to do something about it. In the extreme case, early warning of a serious miscalculation or false assumptions, on which the project was based, may enable the project to be abandoned at minimum cost.

Central control of a project by a project manager means that there is one centre concerned with the economic execution of the project. Like any other manager, the project manager works to a budget. He examines the forecast and actual charge from every department and subcontractor. If a project has no project manager, and is known to be of high priority within the company, departmental managers will be tempted to use it as a milk cow. Their expenditure on the project will be padded to help them conceal the fact that they are overspending elsewhere. They may even charge expenditure on some unauthorised but pet project of their own against the company project. Subcontractors may load on unjustified overheads or even charge twice for the same work. A good project manager prevents this. He holds expenditure to justifiable levels. If budget is exceeded it is for known reasons and not just insidious cost creep.

It may be argued that if all he is doing is preventing unauthorised cross-charging that this is not very productive. The cost would be incurred just the same and the only effect of the project manager is to generate more paper argument plus his own costs. We believe this is not so. If there is proper budgetary control over the normal activities of departments in the company, the project manager is preventing the use of the project budget as an escape hatch and is actually keeping cost down and preventing unnecessary expenditure. He forces departmental managers to think about their charges to the project and not just take the easy way out.

## 2:4   TIMELINESS

A major benefit of project management is the greater likelihood of the project being completed on time. Most companies and government concerns grossly underestimate the effects of delay in completion of project. By having a rolling completion date rather than a fixed date for completion, the real extent of the delay may not be appreciated. The fact that many projects are weeks or months late is a commonplace. Some projects are literally years late in completion. Disbelievers should refer to the Sydney Opera House, a well-documented case of project delay. Without project management, project delay is most frequently not the result of trading-off improved performance and reduced cost against some extra time. More commonly the delay goes hand in hand with vastly increased cost and sometimes with reduced performance as well.

Nearly always delayed completion of a project results in heavy overrun costs. We have already referred to the cost of financing the capital employed in delayed projects. There is also the cost of disruption. Any large project consists of a whole network of activities which have a logical connection with each other. Delay on one activity may result in resources for another activity being held up and kept idle till the first activity is completed. To take a simple case, bricklayers cannot erect the walls of a conventional house until the foundations are ready. In simple cases it may be possible to employ the bricklayers on another job till the foundations are ready. But even in this case there are some costs involved in rescheduling and transferring work from one site to another. In more involved cases in a large company, the costs of redeployment or the cost of idle resources may get lost—but they are real costs just the same. Where subcontractors are involved one may be sure that the extra costs will be firmly placed on the table. In many cases it is just not possible to redeploy resources at short notice. If a project manager cannot completely avoid delay he can at least forecast it well in advance, thus making redeployment of resources more practicable.

Perhaps the two largest costs due to delay are the fact that income generated from the completed project is delayed and opportunities, have to be foregone because resources are tied up in the uncompleted project. In most cases there is a straightforward relationship between delay in completion and delay in receipt of income. In the case of the London Airport Cargo EDP Scheme (LACES) with which we were concerned, the National Data Processing Service calculated that they would lose £3 revenue for every minute the project was delayed. In practice, of course, delay in completion would have been in units of days rather than minutes. Nonetheless it was a figure firmly in the minds of those concerned and helped to concentrate their minds.

There may, of course, be cases where the cost of delay is more onerous. The date of completion of project may be related to an ideal date for putting the product of the project into use. This may be related to some seasonal factor or to patterns of trade. If the due date is missed by a week, it may mean a delay not just of a week in putting the result into operation but perhaps a month, three months or even a year. The cost in terms of lost revenue can be frighteningly large. There are some cases, for instance a new oil refinery, where even if the project is not completed on time, some degraded use can still be obtained from that part of the refinery which is complete. These are, of course, factors of which management are aware whether or not they have a project manager. However, a project manager is more continuously aware of them. They are factors which he takes into account when evaluating possible trade-offs. The project manager should, at the least, complete a project more nearly to time than would be done without a project manager.

The opportunities foregone because of delay or overspending on a project can be the most damaging cost. Staff and resources fully committed on one project cannot be committed to another until they are released from the first. A delayed project or worse still a project the completion date of which cannot be forecast means that opportunities must be allowed to slip by.

In summary, the benefits that come from project management are all those you would expect from the fact that the project is looked at as a whole by one central controlling intelligence rather than being looked at by dozens of managers for whom it represents only a minor part of their activities. Project management should provide realistic project plans and the timely and effective execution of those plans. Successful project management will result in projects completed on time, within budget and to the performance standards set. The fact that many project managers produce results short of this standard is not a condemnation of project management—the results would probably have been far worse without project management.

In some industries, the cost of project management is recognised and allowed for at the planning stage of the project. Indeed a project team may be appointed almost from the moment when the project ceases to be an idea and starts to be planned. In other industries or companies project management is an entirely new concept. Here top management may look askance at the costs of project management. These costs can be clearly seen, while in the early heady days of the project there may be no reason to expect that problems will arise. However, all experience suggests that no large project goes exactly according to plan without problems. There certainly will be problems and the larger the number of parties involved and the greater the complexity of the project the more and worse will those problems be.

Although we are firm believers in project management we recognise that there may be duplication of effort, where project team staff merely repeat or monitor the work done by line management in the main departments. This is most likely to occur where only a few departments of the company are involved in the project—however, as the number of departments increases so the straight duplication in project team effort drops. There is also the possibility that the appointment of a project manager instead of easing the flow and progress of the project may just create friction. Indeed we have come across some project managers who deliberately set out to create conflict and distrust between departments, contributing to their project. This is a practise that we cannot condemn too strongly. The company continues after completion of the project and it is no part of the project manager's job to sow dissension which will last beyond the life of his project.

Another area of concealed project management cost is the cost of assembling and dispersing the project team. If a project is to get off to a flying start it may be necessary to recruit staff before the final decision to go ahead is taken. The decision to recruit or transfer staff may prove to be premature. The decision to go ahead may be delayed or it may even be decided that the project should not proceed. The problem is, however, greater at the completion end. There may be a tendency to hold the project team together at the end of the project. At first this is justified by the need to tie up loose ends. Later perhaps the team is held together so that they may be available for the next project that comes up. If a project lasts for two years and the project team is kept together as a charge on the project for a further year before they are reallotted to other duties, this represents a considerable addition to the project management costs.

Senior management may be forgiven for seeing the costs of project management as a concrete cost to be added to the budgeted cost of the project whereas the benefits and savings may appear nebulous. Perhaps the project will be on time and within budget without incurring project management costs. Perhaps if it does go late and overrun the budget, this might have happened just the same even if project management costs had been incurred. In real life experience suggests that project management does succeed in putting projects to bed in a more timely and effective way than if they are left to normal line management and committee control. If you wonder about justifying the cost just work out the full true cost to your company of each month of delay in a project completion date.

## 2:5  CUSTOMER SATISFACTION

With central control of a project coupled with the right leadership, policies, procedures, techniques and management tools, the best possible groundwork is laid for project success. In fact the complexity of modern advanced technology projects makes it quite certain that they could not be brought to a successful conclusion without project management. However, success means two things: first, that the customer is satisfied that the task has been completed how and when it should have been—the completed project has to work to the agreed specification, to be on time and to be at the agreed price plus or minus any agreed changes; second, the supplier has to make a fair profit and to feel too that the job has been successful for him. Business is built in the majority of cases on sound customer satisfaction. By properly applied project management one is using the management tools to ensure customer satisfaction, the key to sustained good business.

# Part Two

# PEOPLE AND PROJECTS

# 3

# Project Manager

*A man so various*
*that he seemed to be not one, but all mankind's epitome*

There is no surer prescription for project failure than the selection of an inadequate project manager. In this chapter we shall discuss the qualities required in a project manager. One rather acid comment made about our book *Successful Project Management* was: "When suggesting how project managers might fit into possible organisation structures they might leave some room for a managing director." There are some people who think of a project manager as a mere progress chaser or someone passively measuring progress on a project and reporting on it. We believe that a project manager is far more than this. He is identified with his project as a captain is identified with his ship. He steers his project through the inevitable squalls and storms into the harbour of successful completion. He does not usurp the authority of the managing director but his attitudes to his project are very similar to the attitudes of a managing director to his company.

By this we do not intend to exaggerate the importance of the project manager. Rather we want to point to the need for him to have a broad approach to his project rather than a narrow functional one. He must carry in his mind throughout his project a picture of that project as it will finally exist when all phases are complete. In broad terms he must know how the parts will fit together to form the whole. This lies at the heart of the project manager's job. The man who is a first rate specialist or an effective functional manager may not make an effective project manager for this very reason. This ability, to see the concrete whole at a time when reality consists of only a few pages defining the objectives of the project, is not all that common. It is akin to the vision of an architect or composer. The architect is probably unable to lay a brick or plaster a wall but he can create a building, which is both useful and beautiful. A composer may not be a trombonist, or a cellist; he may not even be able to hear the music he composes yet he may create music that will be played for generations. The architect understands building. The composer understands music. So the project manager may not himself require to possess any of the detailed skills that are required for his project. He must, however, have the same vision of the whole and the same understanding of the interaction of the parts as the architect or composer.

If the project manager is a specialist of some kind, he must be careful not to spend an undue amount of his time on his speciality. Perhaps he regards himself as a top fractional motor designer. Perhaps his £5 million project required £5000 worth of fractional motors. It is natural that he will be interested in which motors are chosen and why. However, he may go beyond that and personally make a detailed assessment of the requirement. He may even decide that no commercially available motor quite meets the need and proceed to modify one or do a redesign from scratch. This can be completely disastrous. In this case it would of course be disastrous because it is a typical case of the expert hunting for excellence without regard to time or cost. It is also disastrous because the time the project manager spends on the interesting aspects of his technical speciality is not being spent on his primary job.

The project manager is appointed to manage. He is required to exercise management skills rather than the skills of the technician or professional man. This does not mean that you can happily move a project manager from a mining project to a hotel building or a computer project. He does need a good working background in the appropriate industry. Indeed at the bottom end of the project scale he may need quite a considerable amount of industry-based skill. As the size and complexity of the project increases so does the need for specific industry skills decline and the need for management skills combined with a broad knowledge of the industry increase. Figure 3.1 illustrates this. Combined with the ability to carry a broad picture of the project in his mind, the project manager is above all someone who gets things done. Project managers approach the problem of getting things done in many different ways. They range from the slave driver, who forces everyone on the project to work, to the persuader, who convinces people of the logic of his proposals and cajoles them to bend their efforts to ensure

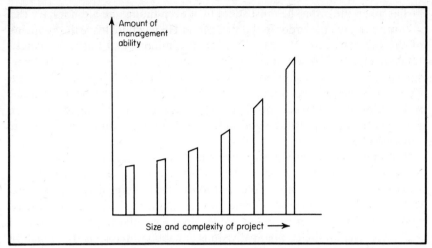

**Figure 3.1** PROJECT SIZE AND COMPLEXITY AND PROJECT
MANAGER ABILITIES

the project's success. In the modern industrial climate of large companies and powerful trade unions the latter is the commoner style.

It is very easy to allow a state of affairs to develop where there is an excuse for everything. Completion dates are delayed, performance characteristics are not met and costs soar. Anyone with experience in industry— or government—is familiar with the picture. The successful project manager is not an excuse maker. He must accept responsibility for the actions of his team and must fully identify himself with his project. All projects are accompanied by problems, shortages of resources, mistakes and faults of all kinds. The project manager needs determination to overcome the problems. He also needs a certain kind of flexible problem-solving mind to enable him to see the way in which the problems can be overcome.

## 3:1   INTEGRITY AND AUTHORITY

Integrity is an old-fashioned word. Yet it is a quality which the project manager must possess. This is not only in the sense of taking full responsibility for his own mistakes and those of his team. He must also be a man on whom his colleagues working on the project can rely. If he gives an instruction by phone to put work in hand, he must accept full responsibility for that just as much as if he had completed a work order and signed it. If he has given the order, he must stand by it even though he did not have the authority to give the order in the first place. He must not leave the recipient of the order to carry the can. This seems a minor point but is absolutely fundamental to project management. The importance of clear written specifications and instructions with a tight change control procedure cannot be stressed too often. Nonetheless the time comes in most large or complex projects where prompt action is essential. If the project manager is trusted this action will be got under way a lot more quickly than would otherwise be the case.

The line manager in industry normally has a well-defined job with clear authority over all who work for him. The project manager is in a different situation and many of the people who contribute to his project will not work directly under his authority. There is often confusion over this question of authority. The authority is not gained by being placed in a position of authority over all the company divisions or subcontractors as this is clearly not possible. The loyalty of those who work for line managers and sub-contractors must intrinsically be to their own managers. Subcontractors and operating divisions may make a large contribution to a project yet their contribution may represent only a small percentage of their own total effort. The project manager is placed in charge of the "project." It is the "project" authority that exists. Fayol uses the following approach in defining a manager's authority as distinct from position or "official" authority [Henri Fayol (1841–1925) wrote *General and Industrial Management*, a well known and recognised "first" to list the principles of management]:

> Authority is the right to give orders and the power to exact obedience. Distinction must be made between a manager's official authority deriving from office, and *personal authority*, compounded of intelligence, experience, moral worth, ability to lead, past services, etc, . . . personal authority is the indispensable complement of official authority.

A job as project manager may also give direct control over some resources, e.g. a project staff, but fundamentally it is an indirect control where powers and influence are manifest from the job description as project manager. Thus, the project manager's authority is a combination of *de jure* and *de facto* elements in the total project environment. In this context the authority has no organisational or functional constraints but diffuses throughout and beyond the organisation, seeking out the ideas and the people it needs to influence. In this way the project manager's effective authority vastly exceeds any that could be simply delegated under the concepts of purely functional authority.

In summary, project authority depends heavily on the personality of the project manager and how he sees his role in relation to the project environment. The project manager is in a focal position in the project endeavours which allows him to control and enhance the flow of information and to have superior knowledge of the project. Authority in the project environment flows horizontally, diagonally and vertically. Technical competence, persuasion, negotiation, reciprocity, alliance and the resolution of deliberate conflict are some of the means that a project manager probably has to use to augment his legal authority to accomplish project objectives.

Thus, effective authority of the project manager is political as well as hierarchical. It also embraces the power to say no and exercise that sanction until investigations as to "why" have been completed. In all these circumstances it may take considerable skill and persuasiveness in the project manager to ensure that the work for his project gets the attention it requires. Also, by their very nature, large and complex projects call for contributions from many—maybe hundreds or thousands—of separate divisions or firms. To persuade all these parties to pull in the same direction and to keep rivalries and jealousy under control calls for considerable skill in the management and organisation of people.

The project manager has of course to be able to deal with people at all levels from the managing director of his own and other companies to the salesman and unskilled labourer as well as highly qualified technicians and specialists.

With all the emphasis on vision, determination and handling people, we may have built up a picture of a "seat of the pants" manager. Yet nothing could be further from the truth. This must be clear from our earlier explanation of the reasons for project management. The need for a project manager arises largely from risk, uncertainty and complexity. These can only be coped with by a meticulous attention to detail and the application of modern project management techniques. We do not expand on these techniques at this point as they are fully covered in other parts of this book and also in our earlier book, *Successful Project Management*. It is sufficient to say here that every project manager should have a critical path network for his project and a system for measuring progress and expenditure against budget.

## 3:2  USE AND RECRUITMENT

We have so far discussed the project manager largely in terms of discrete projects, where he is appointed at or near the start of a project and sees it through. However, project managers are used quite commonly in industry and commence in slightly different circumstances. This is when some situation has got into a mess and special measures are required to put it right. An example is where a firm is using a computer and for some reason or reasons is not getting the benefits that were expected from it. In these circumstances the situation may be investigated and a project manager appointed to ensure that the necessary actions actions are taken to rectify the situation.

Where do project managers come from and how are they trained? This can be a very serious question for firms that have not previously used project management. It can also be a problem for firms that are significantly extending the use of project management. Ideally project managers should be found from within the firm. It may be practicable to recruit a project manager from outside for a project with a long timescale. However, experience suggests that most projects are undertaken on a tight timescale with no time to waste. A project manager recruited from outside will spend a large part of his first few weeks and months in finding his way around the firm. He will not only have to find his way around the formal organisation, but will also have to learn the informal organisational and who the people are who will really get things done for him. He will have to learn about the company's policies and procedures, its trade links and practices. He will have to get to know people. All this takes time. Worse than the passage of time is the possibility that an error made in ignorance in the early stages of a project may have serious repercussions later.

In recruiting project managers from within the firm there are certain problems to be faced. First of all, and particularly if the firm has not used project management before, there may be suspicion of the whole idea. People are likely to say: "The idea sounds fine, but a project by definition has a limited life cycle. What happens to the project manager at the end of the project?" The easy answer is that he will move smoothly onto the next project—naturally a large and more important one. However in real life, projects do not neatly follow one after the other. There is normally a gap, in which it is necessary to keep the project manager gainfully employed, or there is a serious overlap. In this case a new project manager may have to be found before the first can be released—thus making the problem of finding a home for the project manager on completion of his project even worse.

On projects with a high technology content it is quite common to make a skilled technologist the project manager. He faces a special problem. This is particularly the case if the project lasts for several years, as many advanced projects do. If the project manager does his job and concentrates on managing the project, he will gradually lose touch with advances in his own technological field. This will happen even though the project itself employs advanced technology in that field. Inevitably his technical knowledge will become obsolescent.

Another approach is to see a spell as a project manager as one of the steps in a career path. If junior managers know that before they can become divisional managers, they will have to have successfully managed one of the firm's projects, there is likely to be no shortage of volunteers. However, even managers tend to be cynical. They may feel that this is just the latest personnel department fad and that by the time they complete the project it will have been forgotten, that no one will be prepared to move over to make room for them and that someone else with no management experience will be promoted to divisional manager over their heads while they are deeply involved in the project and cannot be released.

In looking for a project manager it is necessary to look for a good manager who has a future in the firm. He must be someone with a flexible approach who can adapt himself quickly to change. A poor-quality manager may get by in a line management appointment because the system will carry and support him for quite a long time before he is found out. This is particularly so, if he was originally competent but just gradually deteriorated on the job. In project management the ill effects of bad management show up quite quickly. It is essential therefore to avoid the temptation of appointing as project manager the person who everybody can spare.

There are some places where one should look automatically for project managers. Young managers who have developed fast but are blocked in the promotion stakes by older men, may prove a fertile recruiting ground. If two departments are to be merged, perhaps the younger of the two managers can be made available to become a project manager.

It may be said that the firm just has no managers to spare and in any case none of them have project management experience, so you must go outside the firm to recruit. Experience suggests that a great many companies—at least in Britain—are overstaffed with managers. We would be sceptical if told that any medium to large firm could not spare a suitable manager to be trained as a project manager.

Not much in the way of formal training for project management is available. There are plenty of courses on the better-known project management techniques such as PERT and discounting techniques of project evaluation. When it comes to training in project management there are very few. Two we know of—because we have lectured on them—are the summer school of the Institute of Electrical Engineers and the Successful Project Management courses of Business Education and Training Services.

For some very large projects more than one project manager may be involved. For instance, it is not uncommon on a large computer project, for the customer to appoint a project manager, and for the main contractor and each of the major subcontractors also to appoint their own project managers. Each such project manager has responsibility within his firm for the project. A subcontractor's project manager as well as having responsibility within his own firm for the successful implementation of their part of the project will also be responsible for interfacing to the main contractor's project manager.

Where a project is very large indeed—as with the Apollo space project and certain new aircraft projects—the project may well be broken up into a number of smaller projects each with its own project manager. All these project managers are co-ordinated and kept in touch by a super-project manager, sometimes known as a program manager.

### 3:3  JOB DESCRIPTION

The following job description was based upon that for a project manager employed by a computer manufacturer to implement a complex project. Although it refers to a particular case and a particular industry it contains much common ground for other industries. We have cut out some items only pertaining to the computer project.

### 3:4  JOB PURPOSE

Responsibility for the successful implementation of the project (system, product or process).

### 3:5  MAIN RESPONSIBILITIES

**1**  To develop the best possible understanding of the customer's functional requirements so as to ensure that they have been correctly interpreted and that the system is designed to be cost effective in terms of standards for performance, quality, reliability, and maintainability which must be agreed with the customer, own company operating divisions and subcontractors. Such requirements must then be configured into standard products and/or into special products that have been endorsed by management in line with company overall policy, both technical and commercial.

**2**  To co-ordinate the use of company resources in order to achieve customer satisfaction, by meeting all agreed customer objectives in a timely and businesslike manner.

**3**  To establish acceptance criteria, the use of which will show between the company and the customer that the company has carried out all its technical obligations.

**4** To plan the whole project task, identify all activities, their timescales, the risks, any necessary backup plans, and the resources necessary to successfully implement the proposal in accordance with the functional requirements. To prepare, with the customer, a basic planning network for all significant activities and their timescales after obtaining agreement on company activities with the appropriate management in the company and with any subcontractors.

**5** To review these plans regularly and take action to recover slippages or to minimise their effects upon the total project.

**6** To propose to management the resources that will be needed to achieve the agreed time plan.

**7** To prepare a project budget profit and loss account covering the total project, from conception to completion. This must be maintained and progressed. All budgets and accounts must be signed off by sales, program management or other departments, as necessary.

**8** To ensure that all "special requirements," are "raised" at the earliest opportunity, where necessary with supporting functional specifications when approved. These special requirements must be reflected into the basic planning network.

**9** To ensure that appropriate design and manufacturing departments correctly interpret the special requirements, and that they are up-dated if changes occur.

**10** Ensuring that appropriate buying instructions, or other instructions are issued to manufacturing, and or development departments.

**11** To ensure that the project has been technically and commercially vetted by the appropriate authority in the company.

**12** To liaise closely with the sales executive so as to ensure that sales management is aware of situations that may affect sales strategy, both short and long term.

**13** To ensure in conjunction with his sales management and comptroller that the contract is one that is acceptable to the company and, prior to the draft contract, the project manager must ensure that any variance to any standard contract terms are acceptable and checked with sales, commercial and technical management, and legal advisers.

**14** To assist in the preparation of any project approval forms required supported by all appropriate appendices and financial details that clearly indicate the profitability of the project and the basis on which these details have been carried out. In addition to this to state clearly all foreseeable problem areas (risks) with recommendations on how these risks may be avoided or minimised, and the implications.

**15** To establish comprehensive and formal change procedures to ensure that any changes and requirements that affect the project are dealt with quickly through the proper channels by agreement with the customer, the company and any subcontractors. To ensure that such agreed changes are properly costed and, if it is appropriate, paid for by the customer.

**16** To ensure that suitable staff are obtained for the project. To prepare job descriptions and terms of reference for the project team covering the following stages:

*a*    Pre-sales (if applicable)
*b*    Implementation
*c*    Post-implementation (e.g. during maintenance and operations)

**17** To manage the team directly answerable to him in order to achieve all the requirements of the project.

**18** To make sure that any project staff reporting to him are adequately trained, that their future career development needs are satisfied and to assist them to make a satisfying move from this project to another task when the appropriate time arrives.

**19** To develop a co-operative spirit with the customer so that user action can be sought where necessary to meet agreed objectives.

**20** To hold regular meetings with the customer to ensure that he is not only aware of the company progress on his project, but is given the necessary guidance in preparing himself for using efficiently the system as from the "ready for service" date. This work will include not only the operational aspects of running the project, training staff, etc, but preparation of building and site in conjunction with company environmental planning staff if appropriate. It will also cover maintenance aspects to meet serviceability requirements.

**21** To identify problems requiring support on or off site, and to solve these problems by action resulting from discussing with appropriate line and support management, whether legal, engineering, systems, or of any other appropriate discipline. Furthermore, to ensure that company departments committed to assisting the project are fully aware of what is required of them and to monitor their progress on such items through the appropriate line and support management.

**22** To report regularly to the appropriate sales management (and other authorities as arranged) on progress and trends for the future progress.

**23** To identify the stage at which handover of the project can be effected to the standard sales support function and to see that this transition is efficiently carried out.

**24** To obtain from the customer agreement that the contractor has carried out his obligations under the contract and in accordance with the acceptance criteria.

**25** To ensure that appropriate procedures, policies and standards are established and can be maintained to guarantee continued customer satisfaction.

**26** To ensure that all objectives and policies are continuously reviewed and updated to meet customer satisfaction requirements.

**27** Maintain awareness of customer attitudes, customer desires and any other factors that could affect the project.

# 4

# Project Team

Many projects are small enough—or sufficiently simple in concept—to be managed by one man or by one man and his secretary. However, large and complex projects tend to need a project management team rather than a single project manager. In these cases, one of the first and most important tasks of a project manager is the selection of his project team. The project team works virtually as an extension of the project manager. It is therefore essential that it is kept small and compact. Each member of the team must know what is in the project manager's mind. He acts in the light of that knowledge. Indeed one might say that the members of a project team must be very close to each other in understanding and live in one another's minds.

## 4:1 BUILDING THE TEAM

The project manager looks at the tasks in front of him and breaks them down in a logical pattern to decide on the ideal team structure for the job. In doing this he must be aware of his own limitations and weaknesses.

There may sometimes be a great temptation to fill a project team with people with the same background and ideas as the project manager. This is a mistake and should be resisted. Team members should be complementary. The job of project management is of course a management job not a specialist's. Yet each project involves certain specialist areas of knowledge and those specialist areas must be covered in the composition of the team.

There is always some conflict between keeping the team as small as possible and providing the ability to handle problem areas in depth. If the team is too small, individuals have to cover too wide a span of control and may not get to grips with problems soon enough. On the other hand, a large team loses cohesion and may break up into factions rather than work as a single coherent team. Each team member should have a job description with a clear purpose and well-defined tasks to be accomplished. However, as the project progresses there is likely to be a considerable fluidity and job descriptions must be kept under constant review to keep them in line with the needs of the project. Particular care must be taken to frame the job purpose so as to provide adequate guidance to enable the job holder to decide his course of action sensibly and constructively when unexpected circumstances arise.

Some project managers like to build up a heirarchical structure within their team with only two or three people in the team reporting directly to them. We do not favour this. Wherever possible we prefer a flat structure with all project team members reporting directly to the project manager. However, on very large projects this may not be possible. In this case an attempt may be made to group staff so as to provide subteams around each of the main members of the project team. A particular problem arises where there is a large number of subcontractors. Particularly on large construction projects there may be literally hundreds of subcontractors. There is a case here for trying to impose a form of cascade project management. In other words, the work to be subcontracted is cut up into a maximum of six main slices each of which is let out on a main subcontract. The problem of breaking this work up between other contractors and providing project management for the slice is then effectively delegated to the slice subcontractor. This helps to limit the size of the main contactor's project team.

When it comes to the point of selecting the actual people for the project team great care must be taken. It is here that company personnel staff must set out to help. In an ideal world, the project manager would provide the personnel department with a specification of each person he needed. The personnel department would tell their computer, which would respond with a list of suitable names. Regretably few firms have such well-organised personnel departments. The major danger to the project manager is that the first offering of staff made to him will be the misfits, who line management are trying to off-load. It does not of course follow that a man who is a misfit in a line department will necessarily be a misfit on a project. We know of one case, where a project manager staffed his project almost entirely with misfits and got excellent results. He did it with his eyes open, recognising why they were misfits in their current jobs and tailoring their jobs on the project team with considerable care so that the job matched the man in each case. Some people are seen by line managers as undisciplined, long haired or too keen to question instructions and established ways of doing things. Some good project staff may be found from amongst such misfits. However, it is necessary to avoid collecting those who are just passengers in their existing job.

When selecting staff, the project manager should not rely solely on the personnel department. He should use his own knowledge of people in his company and make full use of his informal contacts, both to check on people offered to him and also to find names of possibles for investigation. In particular, if we want a specialist of some sort, we normally start our search by chatting with our friends in the specialist area to throw up possible names. We look also to users at the receiving end of specialist services to suggest names. We are not necessarily looking for specialists fully qualified and experienced for the job in hand. Even experts have to start somewhere. So we look for someone with adequate experience and potential. We look for people who in particular have a background of getting things done rather than people with a reputation for theorising. In most cases the project should offer each team member an opportunity to broaden or deepen his experience rather than being apparently a chance to do the same as last time. This helps to keep him mentally alert and provide a degree of additional motivation.

In discussing jobs in your project team with potential team members, be cautious of the stresses the project will impose on them and do not attempt to conceal the difficulties that will arise. When you take people into your project team you want to keep them for the duration of the project. In a two-year project you will lose a lot of mementum if you lose half your project team at the end of the first year. So discuss with them in particular the periods of absence from home that are likely to be involved. Discreetly try to draw them out on their family and social commitments. The man who turns out to have family commitments, which make it imperative that he is at home every Saturday and Sunday, is a dead loss when weekend work becomes necessary.

Once you have identified the staff you want you have the problem of securing their services. This may be straight forward, but if you have picked good people, there may well be objections from their existing managers or there may be other managers in the company competing for their services. These are circumstances when the project manager must really be prepared to fight for what he wants. If there is one man he really feels he must have for his project team, then he should fight right up the management tree to get him. Having said that, we must recognise that it is very rare for one man to be so utterly indispensible that there is no acceptable substitute. The success of your project—and your reputation depends on the people in your project team so it is well worth the effort to secure the right people.

In practice, as you start to assemble your team, some compromise is necessary. You will find some good people you want to have on the team who do not quite meet the job specification or who overlap two jobs rather than fitting either of them. It generally pays to modify your project team organisation rather than insist on filling the precise jobs you first thought of. In any case, time is normally of the essence in assembling the project team. Also as the project progresses the work load will shift between jobs and require some adjustment to the boundary between them. This perhaps emphasises the need for flexibility in the people chosen.

Project team is not just an idle expression. A project team really must function as a team. They must cover each other's weaknesses, rely on each other's strengths and be prepared to fill in or cover each other in periods of absence or serious overload. This means that it is important to consider how the team members will get on together. Will they be compatible? Will they work easily together? Or will they continually rub each other up the wrong way? A project team may last for a shorter period than a marriage but the ability to get on together and to live in one another's minds is important. Many members of a project team will be specialists and their specialist knowledge and experience is essential to the performance of their function. However, the primary task of both project manager and team is management. In this sense the team is merely an extension of the project manager who cannot be a superman. Just as the project manager has to avoid becoming bogged down on his pet speciality and concentrate on the management of the project, so must his team do the same. The search for technical excellence is frequently the enemy of the perfectly workable solution which will keep the project moving towards its required conclusion.

In building up your team remember there is a great deal of routine to be attended to. A central register should be kept of all letters. There is the project baseline to be kept up to date and the routine work to be done in connection with the change control procedure. These will be the network to be kept up dated and routine reports to be made. On large projects there is a good case for having an administrator or clerk on the team to relieve the project manager of this routine work.

## 4:2 ON-THE-JOB TRAINING

All projects must to a variable degree be good training grounds for future project managers or senior project staff. The project manager in conjunction with personnel must rate as a high priority the training, on the job, of members of his team. There is the usual difficulty. Everybody is much too busy to train or be trained. There are few projects or other jobs for that matter where such excuses are not laboured. Training must occur, however hard it is to arrange. Some will of course just happen because of having done a particular part of the project task.

The project manager can help in several ways to see that training occurs. He can show by example how certain planning and control activities should be carried out, getting his staff to do as much of this as possible, insisting that the team members report in a manner designed to bring out the real problems, encouraging them to keep up with their basic technical expertise by contact with other experts, learned societies, etc, above all by making them work as a team so that each learns from the other, and by bringing out the best methods and procedures for all to see.

# 5

# Company Personnel Policies for Project Staff

Companies that intend to become project oriented, require positive personnel policies to ensure that they obtain and retain project managers and staff of the required calibre. Specifically policies are required to cover:

1  Quick assembly and dispersal of project teams
2  Holding project staff between projects
3  Contract staff for single projects
4  Relationship between project staff and line management
5  Training, including on the job training, and grading project managers
6  Remuneration policies and performance bonus
7  Working conditions and allowances

## 5:1  ASSEMBLY AND DISPERSAL

Most companies that are involved in many projects will maintain a central department concerned with project evaluation and planning and with the vetting of project proposals produced elsewhere in the company. When a new project receives the approval, this department may have to take initial responsibility for getting the project going until a project manager can be appointed. This is not very satisfactory because, in practice, most projects requiring a project manager, are planned to a very tight timescale. No delay can be afforded in getting the project manager on to the job and providing him with his team.

Any project plan involving the allocation of a considerable number of staff to the project must allow sufficient time to obtain these staff and indoctrinate them. For a large two-year computer programming project, for instance, it would not be unreasonable to allow three to six months for assembly of staff and their familiarisation with the project, project standards and user requirements. However, we are here concerned with the project manager and the small team he needs to help him manage a project. Here there simply is not time to take three to six months assembling the team.

The project manager is really required from day one or preferably earlier. Ideally any proposed project that has a reasonable chance of being approved for execution should have a project manager. This gives rise to problems if a high proportion of project proposals are still-born. It is difficult enough to obtain project managers for projects that are firm goers. It is very much more difficult to persuade the right calibre of man to take over a proposed project that has only a 30% chance of going ahead. One possibility is to earmark prospective project managers in advance. If the appointment is to be seen as a promotion this may be an acceptable way of getting a project manager quickly into the job. In the evaluation stage of the project he can be appointed project manager, designate. His existing manager can make his plans for his replacement in advance. The project manager designate can spend time in inducting his own designated replacement. If the project comes to nothing the project manager carries on with the job that he was in, as does his designated replacement. Even though the project has come to nothing he had been forced to lift his eyes from the day-to-day work of his normal job and it has also given someone else a chance to learn about it. On the debit side, both he and his planned replacement may be unsettled by the procedure. However, he can remain on the transfer list for the next project while continuing his normal job.

Having a project manager designated well in advance of the decision to procede with a project gives great advantages. He becomes familiar with the project and identifies possible problem areas. He starts to meet the people who will be involved in the project in his own company, among the users and among the subcontractors.

Not every firm is prepared to countenance the move of managers between normal line appointments and project management. It is frequently argued that the job characteristics are different. Certainly project managers tend to be younger, tougher and more non-conformist than their opposite-numbers in line management. However, some firms see a spell in project management as ideal training for senior management posts and for posts running subsidiary companies or independent branches. It is also true that many project managers after the strain and stress of two major projects feel that they have proved themselves and would prefer to continue in a line management job rather than start yet another project with all its risks and uncertainties as well as the disruption to normal family and social life.

## 5:2 BETWEEN PROJECTS

Perhaps a more difficult problem even than finding project managers in the first place is what to do with them when they have finished their project. For a time they can be employed in tidying up the loose ends and holding the hand of the line manager who takes over the routine running of the project's product. He can be employed for a while in putting down on paper the lessons he has learnt on the project for the benefit of future project managers in the firm. He can be used to revise the company's project management training courses and to lecture on them. If his project has been a prestige one or one that provides a reference sell for the company's salesmen, then he can do a lot of public relations and sales support lecturing. Sooner or later, if a new project does not come up, the problem comes up, what to do with the project manager?

Companies that wish to make their mark as successful in managing projects must develop a policy for identifying, training and retaining project managers. It is uneconomic to find a potential project manager, train him and give him his head on a major project only to lose him to a competitor because the firm cannot offer him an attractive follow-on job. We believe the best policy is to have a small central pool of project managers. Project manager are drawn from this pool for new projects and return to the pool on completion. The pool is used to hold project managers until either a new project is available or until they can be rotated into a normal line management post. The pool can from time to time be increased by taking in potential project managers both from line management posts and from members of project teams that have shown potential. As well as project managers the pool should hold some of the skilled specialists needed for project teams. For instance, a computer manufacturer providing project management for turn-key real-time computer projects would need some key programming and communications specialists for such projects. Some of these people would form an essential part of the pool.

To be effective the project management pool must do more than just exist, it should perform a profitable job in its own right. The members of the pool can be employed on the tasks already mentioned—sales support, public relations, training and vetting new project proposals. They can also be used as a task force for carrying out investigations of management problem areas and for dealing with disaster situations. They can be used to investigate the practicability of new ideas and to plan ways in which opportunities can be exploited for the firm's profit. In particular they can be used to devise means by which the firm as a whole can benefit from the lessons they learnt on their last project. They should not, however, forget the old adage that "hard cases make bad law." In other words, it may be dangerous to generalise too far from the special circumstances of one particular project.

## 5:3  CONTRACT STAFF

Some firms try to overcome the problem of finding suitable project managers and project team staff by hiring them specially on a contract for one project. They may be satisfactory where a project has a long timescale of several years or where the individual concerned is employed in a consultative capacity during the evaluation stages of the project. However, it is otherwise a fairly dangerous proceeding. However long the timescale for a project, it is usually too short for the work to be done. If the first few months of a project have to be devoted to finding and hiring a project manager, who then has to spend several weeks learning about the project and the company environment, this is an unwarranted use of the time available for the project, except in the most extreme cases. This problem can be mitigated by employing a caretaker project manager from within the firm, but this is rarely satisfactory. Many key decisions are made in the early months of a new project. If a caretaker makes the wrong decisions, he can waste more time than his appointment saves. Similarly many caretakers merely prevaricate, which is an extremely expensive process.

A further problem with the contract project manager is his lack of knowledge of the firm. He can be shown the formal organisation quickly, but it usually takes at least six months to find out how a large organisation really works—or at least to get a rough approximation to the facts. Every organisation has its informal network of contacts. There are ways of getting things done quickly in each department and ways of indefinitely postponing action. A new man can be seriously slowed up till he gets to know the ropes. Apart from this he may find the resultant delays both infuriating and frustrating. He may be tempted to express his views violently and openly. One result of this is normally for him to make enemies who may deliberately set out to hinder him.

A further problem is that of pay and conditions of service. The contract man carries quite a lot of risk and expects to be paid accordingly. His pay has to recognise that as compared with the company man he has to make his own provision for retirement, for longer-term illness and the possibility of periods of unemployment between assignments. Into the bargain, his contract is to cover a period throughout which he will be active and working very long hours. The company man may have several months light running in the pool to follow his successful assignment. The contract man will be out after project acceptance and busy selling himself for his next assignment. The man, who is good enough to be a freelance project manager is normally something of an entrepreneur, who knows his own value. He also knows that once a firm has committed itself to a project, it has an urgent need to get on with it. If he is good at his job and available now, it is worth the firm paying several thousands of pounds extra to obtain his services now rather than wait to find someone cheaper. In consequence good project managers on contract are expensive.

The most risky thing of all about hiring a project manager on a contract for a single project is that you do not know him. However good your personnel selection procedures and however meticulously you pick up his references, you may make a mistake. He may be no good at all. He may just be no good for the particular circumstances of this project. He may have had a past full of achievement but have become tired or started to go to seed. When you are outside a firm it is easier to conceal women, money, drink or drug problems than it is when you are inside it.

Once a project manager has been hired for a specific project he must be given his head and allowed to get on with it. It is normally extremely difficult to make an assessment of how he is doing until he has been at the job for at least six months. In these six months it is possible to do a lot of damage that is not immediately noticeable. If his performance—the progress of his project—is so bad that he has to be fired, then you are back to square one looking for a new project manager. Breaking the contract of the original project manager is likely to prove very expensive. The damage to the project and the consequent cost is likely to be considerable.

A good project manager hired for a single project may have a loyalty to his project and his staff. Most such project managers have their first loyalty to themselves. The one thing that is certain is that their first loyalty will not be to the firm that pays them.

We strongly favour firms finding their project managers from within their own resources. One management pundit is on record as saying that if in any large organisation you line up all the managers in quite random order and fire every other one in the line, the organisation would function just as well if not better. This is a sweeping generalisation, but assuming it contains a few grains of truth, most large organisations should be able to find some spare young managers, who can be trained for project management. This should certainly be so in companies that have an effective management succession plan in operation. If you possibly can, find your project managers internally.

Even if you have to select someone regarded as young and very junior in the organisation, he will probably surprise you by his reaction to responsibility and the project environment.

If you really can't find someone with the required qualities—perhaps because yours is a comparatively small firm—it may be better to look for someone to hire as part of your regular management staff rather than to look for someone on short contract. One source of suitable people is officers retiring from the technical branches of the armed forces, particularly the Royal Engineers. Not every retired officer is an elderly blimp, set in his ways. Many short-service officers decide to make the break in their thirties and they frequently have relevant project experience, even though it may be in a field other than that of your project.

## 5:4   PROJECT–LINE RELATIONSHIPS

The relationship between line and project managers is largely a matter of the latter's personality and approach. It is, however, an area of possible difficulty and friction. Company personnel policies can do something to help. Project managers should be appointed with as much internal publicity as line managers and their right of access to a senior level of management, preferably board level, should be spelt out. If the company publishes a personnel policy manual then it should contain a reference to encouraging the rotation of staff through project teams as well as normal appointments in their speciality.

## 5:5   CONDITIONS AND REWARDS

Working conditions and special allowance for project staff require careful thought. Many projects are implemented in remote places. By remote, we do not mean in darkest Africa, but only that they are remote relative to the normal place of work of people in the firm. The project site may also be sufficiently far from the normal place of work for project staff that they have to live temporarily away from home to be near the site. This may be for the whole life of the project or for only one phase of it. Similarly, project staff may have to live for a time near the premises of subcontractors, particularly when subcontractors are falling behind with their commitments. Most projects go through a phase when weekend working is essential. Many may require work to go on through twenty four hours a day, thus necessitating both the organisation of shifts and the working of long hours. The project manager, in particular, has to be available during normal hours and must also, if he is to perform his essential leadership role, be present for some part of the weekend and night shift working.

This all represents considerable extra effort as well as considerable dislocation to family and social life. This deserves some reward. The reward must not be simply for working long and awkward hours but reward for the results that stem from that effort. Effective project management can, as we have seen, bring very considerable benefits. Not the least of these are financial benefits. Some small part of these benefits should be used to reward those that have made them possible. In general we believe that project staff should be paid salaries that are comparable to line people carrying responsibilities of a similar degree. The extra reward should take the form of a bonus related to the outcome of the project in terms of performance, costs and timescales. The bonus should also pay some regard to the tidiness of completion of the project.

Opinions differ as to whether details of the bonus system should be disclosed at the beginning of the project. Those opposed to disclosure are generally those that are not confident of their own ability to define a bonus scheme that does achieve its objectives without leaving a mass of loop-holes that will enable project staff to milk the company without delivering the goods. We are firmly in favour of announcing the bonus scheme and its terms as soon as possible after the start of the project. If a bonus scheme can be devised that is applicable to all the company's projects then so much the better. The advantage of disclosing the bonus scheme at the beginning of the project is that it can have the effect of a positive incentive to performance rather than be a mere postfacto recognition. One condition for any project bonus scheme should be that no bonus is paid to anyone leaving the project at his own request before his scheduled release date.

Apart from salary there is the question of allowances and expenses. Here the basic rule is: "if in doubt aim on the generous side." Project staff should "live the project" and be thinking about it and its problems for most of their waking hours. They should not be distracted from this by grievances over expenses. If the firm is mean and penny pinching with them, they may feel that their efforts are not appreciated and may well reduce them. In particular if a project forces staff to live away from home, let them live comfortably as close to their work as possible even if that means putting them up at more expensive hotels than staff of their grade would normally be allowed. If they work long hours make sure that hot drinks and snacks are available on site. For manual workers or people working out of doors make sure there are decent rest facilities on site, where they can drink their tea or just take a break in comfort. If necessary, special facilities should be provided for working, bathing, cleaning-up generally and for getting dry. There should of course be adequate lavatory facilities. If staff work overnight or at weekends, there may be few local facilities for taking meals. Make sure they can get meals even if that means you have to arrange access to someone else's night canteen or perhaps hire a cook and set up a kitchen on-site.

Transport to work can also be a problem with remote sites, long hours, night and weekend working. If a man has to make a long-distance journey overnight to meet the project requirements, let him travel first-class with a sleeper. If it will allow him to have an extra night at home with his wife and family then allow him to fly, if it is practicable. If journeys to site can be made more quickly and easily by car than by public transport then give a generous mileage allowance to people who chose to use their cars. Consider laying on your own shuttle service bus or minibus to take staff to and from their hotels or railway terminals. For a large project on a remote site you should consider having project pool cars available on site. These can be used for ferrying people from one part of the site to another, as well as bringing staff in to work and taking them home. Such pool cars can also be used for collection of urgently needed documentation, spares and small tools. Always be generous in making conditions as easy as possible on a project. This applies not just to the project manager and his management team but to all the people assigned to work on the project.

Project managers are busy people but they must never forget that their prime resource is people. The good project manager looks after his people. Company personnel staff must go out of their way to help him and not to hinder him.

## 5:6   TRAINING AND GRADING

In order to set up pay-scales, career structure and training, project managers have to be fitted in to the overall company organisation. There should be an assessment scheme for grading projects in order to find out the type and grade project manager that should be employed. One might decide, for example, that by various standards it is possible to build up such a requirement from a points scheme derived from items as follows:

1   Total size of project (£)
2   Number of direct staff
3   Number of men on-site
4   Number of subcontractors
5   Technical complexity

6 Risks
7 Newness of scheme
8 Special features
9 Customer
10 Market area
11 Company priority—etc

This gives some common ground for the choosing of the appropriate project manager. It is, however, unlikely that the final choice can be entirely based on such criteria. Management may decide to put extra weighting on certain factors for particular projects. From a general grading into, for example, four grades of project manager the grades have to be associated with company pay-scales after examining industry salaries for the type of job.

The question of career structure is important in that people from other activities in the company will want to know what promotion can be achieved in moving to a particular project manager job relative to their own. Similarly a project manager will expect to see promotion paths other than in project management.

Various training courses need to be set up varying from a general course for new project managers to advanced and refresher courses for practising company or recruited project managers. The latter will want a "know the company" type course. In training a powerful aid is "on the job" training. This can be achieved by careful planning of the project support-staff on projects so that they gain the right sort of experience to fit them for bigger and better jobs as well as contribute to the project task. Formal general training could be on the following syllabus lines with special emphasis from a particular industry or company point of view: objectives and concepts; defining a project; planning and scheduling; management and communication; customer relations and satisfaction; commercial items; control policies, procedures and techniques.

*Objectives and concepts*: defining project management—needs and benefits—advantages and disadvantages—company aspects, that is type of industry, type of company, type of project manager, particular problems—general job description—relationships with rest of company—general management environment.

*Defining a project*: assessing customer requirements—advising customers—working with customer requirements—acceptance criteria—finishing definitions—task definition in company terms—project approval process in company—all technical procedures for definitions.

*Planning and scheduling*:   need to plan—planning concepts—strategic and tactical planning—approvals—project analysis—resource planning—planning summary—macronets—PERT charts—outputs—bar charts—surveys and sampling techniques—dangers of inadequate planning—relationships between time, resources, performance and costs.

*Management and communication*:   assessing the manpower requirements—choosing, motivating and keeping an effective project team—helping the customer with staff definitions where appropriate—staff training—progress meetings—management reports—team working, management and delegation—communication basics—progress chasing, staff/live communications—agreeing key dates—motivation and leadership—thought processess, positive thinking, lateral thinking—accountability—authority.

*Customer relations and satisfaction*:   growing a good customer—honesty with the customer—problems face to face—importance of acceptance criteria—helping customer—after project care—maintenance—spares.

*Commercial items*:   contract—importance to project manager—UK and overseas—amendments—penalties or liquidated damages—acceptance criteria—turnkey projects—subcontractors—consortia operation—main contractors risks—basic knowledge of law and readings—business knowledge.

*Control policies, procedures and techniques*:   using management tools of trade-offs—techniques such as PERT, CPM, bar charts, line of balance, statistics etc—financial control—time control—resource control—P & L accounts—change control, documentation, philosophy, costing—filing—commercial control actions—management by exception—plan changing—schedule adjustment—control reports—general control documentation.

Part Three

# PROJECT PLANNING
# AND PROGRESSING

# 6

# Project Plan

It is possible to do without a project plan. There are always quite successful projects conceived on backs of envelopes but invariably they are one man projects. They may be new ideas, simple but brilliant. They are looked after like children by their inventors and developers.

For most of us, however, life is not like that. We are involved in projects of reasonable technological complexity—an ammonia plant, a new town centre, a new factory, computer or bridge, an engineering development, a manufacturing or marketing project, etc. In the bulk of cases it would seem inconceivable if a plan was not produced yet it is all too easy to go on without a really effective plan.

The problem is that short-term planning is easy; long-term planning is not. A series of short-term plans, hooked together as the time goes on, is not a long-term plan. One must sit down at the beginning and prepare the complete long-term plan. The main ingredient of a plan, first and foremost, is a forecast. It might not turn out to be a good forecast, in which case it has to be altered more than one would like. It may have to be changed because of external influences but it is still a forecast of what is most likely to occur or what one ought to do. Some people think of a plan as a map that is prepared on the basis of the best information of previous travellers plus some guesses. There are always many arguments against planning. The strongest is that one does not know for certain what events will occur. Of course not, no one has a crystal ball, but it is surprising how much influence one can bring to bear on a situation if one plans properly towards a major goal and the intermediate steps.

"We cannot afford the effort," this is another strong plea from the anti-planning lobby. We argue that with all the risks inherent in any undertaking, especially technical tasks, one cannot afford *not* to plan. Examples abound of company fortunes adversely affected because of lack of planning on projects. Planning is thinking deeply through a problem, examining all the logical paths, putting together the various detailed tasks that make up the complete job and writing down all the items in their logical and time order. From this complete examination of the task will come:

1    The timing of all the component parts and the total project time
     After this can come the refining process of endeavouring to adjust the
     parts to fit an end date requirement until the plan is optimum
2    The costs, budget and profit and loss account
3    The complete definition of the project

As time passes the plan needs revision, in fact the revision is continuous, but the structure exists so that the original aims, logic of approach and timing is there to see and build upon.

Another simple but powerful reason for planning stems from communication needs. A common plan for all to see is an inspirational item. It is an aligning object; a common ideal for all the project staff to observe and work to.

An anology which seems to us particularly apt regarding the planning of a project is a ship's voyage. It is possible to take a ship to sea without planning of any description and get somewhere. It is possible to start a project in the same way and get somewhere. Compare a complicated project with a long voyage through difficult waters. Most people would admit the foolishness of starting the voyage without very thorough planning but people embark on complex projects without the same caution. One of the problems with management generally is that it looks easy and project management seems just another form of management. If one pays the same attention to the planning of a project as famous sailors have to planning their voyages then one will have the best chance of success.

6:1  ELEMENTS OF THE PLAN

With the voyage the first question is: "Where are we going?" With the project plan the question is similar: "What are we setting out to achieve?" The initial answer may be just a few words, after that we can start to break down the complete journey.

This first phase of project planning is called "task definition." It is a vital phase and should cover the entire scope of the project task.

## 6:2  KEY QUESTIONS

These must be asked as one goes through the task definition and are based on the following:

1   Is it known precisely what the customer wants ("customer" can also mean another part of a company in the case of internal projects)?
2   Is it certain that what the customer says he wants is really what he wants or needs? Can he be advised in this? Is there any danger of a misunderstanding (it is incredible what misunderstandings do occur in what one might call simple issues)?
3   Is it a "standard" task—i.e. has it been done before, preferably more than once?
4   Are there new developments required? Are these brand new—i.e. a new "state of the art," or are they developments of an already existing process or design?
5   Are there *any* areas of the task that are not quite clear or cannot be visualised in advance? If so one must work away at these until a sufficiently clear picture emerges of the whole task
6   Can the risks inherent in performing the task be defined?
7   Is the good project a "good" thing to do for the company and can the reasons be detailed?
8   Can a tolerance be set with confidence on the project overall cost budget and time plans?
9   Can acceptance tests be defined so that the supplier and customer have a clear end to the job, giving customer satisfaction, on the one hand and job planning clarity and, hopefully, profitability to the supplier on the other?

From each of the questions, and further questions arising from them, will come definitive answers such that a complete project definition will emerge covering all the facets of the task—that is the customer requirement matched by:

1   Complete task specification highlighting in a special report any area which is not completely specifiable at the time
2   Budgeted costs and projected profit and loss account for the project including tolerances

3    Special report on any areas of risk which could cause loss of money or customer dissatisfaction

4    Specification of acceptance tests which will prove agreeable to both supplier and customer

5    Management report embracing the above key items and including considered statements on the likely contractual arrangements, usefulness of the project to the company, and effects on present and future business

6    A "macronet" or small network diagram of the significant activities (this will be expanded later into the overall network of the project— see the examples in Chapter 7)

To prepare the complete project definition management and industrial technical knowledge is called for. We cannot help in the second item, expect for computers; the object of this book is to help with project management. On the management side we must make sure we deal with all the facets that can bear on the project. Apart from the actual industry required to cover the technical aspects of the definition, there are seven other main issues it is neccessary to examine in the utmost detail as part of the planning: resources, timescales, quality and reliability, value analysis, costs, contractual aspects, and progressing.

## 6:3   RESOURCES

The project plan is entirely dependent on the resources that can, or will, be employed. Whether the task should be carried out at all is always an important commercial issue. It may, or may not be, good for the company to do it. The resources necessary have to be assessed. In general, resources can be broken down into the following areas:

1    Manpower
2    Finance
3    Materials (raw and finished)
4    Space, services, tools and machinery

In the case of those projects where standard equipment is being assembled to form a system or whole end structure, some of the resource complications may not occur if the project is considered as being the final "putting together"—for example, a very standard computer system or an "off-the-shelf" factory. Immediately a departure from standard occurs, or the project is considered to be an earlier phase—for example, the design, development and manufacturing of what ultimately becomes a standard item, then it is certain that all items within the resources will be utilised. In any complex project—for example, a non-standard computer system, a civil engineering project or any large engineering project, again, all resource items will come into play. At this stage one should look at the effect on the plan (or vice versa) as far as resources are considered. The next main item to be considered after resources will be time plans, and immediately an interaction is apparent.

It is clear that if an activity takes ten weeks to carry out the statement is incomplete without saying what manpower, tools, services, materials, cost budget and space will be required to allow it to happen. Conversely, if there are constraints on any of the resources the timescale is almost bound to be affected. You may easily at this juncture say how simple all this is, how obvious the interrelationships are. The facts on how many projects are run badly, because these interrelationships are not studied and put into practice, give a different picture. Obvious or not, they are, like so many other management simplicities, just simply not done or inadequately done. Herein lies the danger. Equally, managers have to judge what, at a particular time, they will accept even though they know that further complications exist and more work has to be done.

*Manpower.* While a particular industry has its own technical and management problems a project manager should find advantage in getting to know as much as possible about resource analysis in terms of manpower, especially on large contracts with many men. The technique it is argued becomes ineffective because manpower is so unpredictable and therefore decisions must always be *ad hoc*. This is the reason why resource analysis should be employed, not why it should not be. Even if apparently *ad hoc* decisions do have to be made because this or that man or men have not turned up for work it is better to make such decisions from as much knowledge as possible. Resource analysis even in a simple form of handworked charts help to show the effects of more or less manpower. When used in conjunction with time analysis it can be a powerful tool. The sort of simple charts in general use are exemplified in Figure 6.1.

After drawing the staff requirements as illustrated or listing them in some other way per period from the task accomplishment plan, the aim is to rationalise the requirements so that the most economic quantities are in use consistant with ensuring the tasks get done. In Figure 6.1, for example, it might be possible to cut back the peaks (shaded) in weeks 3, 5 and 6 and 11, in order to employ no more than 5 or 6 of this type of staff. It may be appropriate to fill in the troughs in weeks, 1, 2 or 7. The saving in this case is only

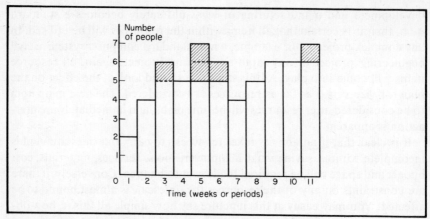

Figure 6.1 MANPOWER CHART FOR ONE TYPE OF TASK

part of the story—it may be more significant to think where the 2 extra men are coming from just for week 5. A stable number of men is easier to arrange. If, in a large job, a real attempt is made to do this the movements and plans to achieve the rationalising of numbers also helps considerably when a labour problem suddenly looms up in one area. Some immediate planning can be done to minimise the problem and practical methods such as outlined become valuable.

In projects using PERT (see next chapter), there are means for the computer to do a large part of the juggling but the manager must eventually choose what he considers to be the most equitable solution. The factors involved may be essentially, availability of certain trades, certain subcontractors and of course the interaction with timescales.

*Finance.* How much of the subject of finance the project manager will ultimately get involved in varies considerably. It is probably true to say that the majority of project managers work in a matrix system of management and that most of the financial aspects are dealt with by line management. By this we mean the problems of providing finance, overall profitability decisions, actual payment of staff, etc. However, the project responsibility is vested in the project manager. He must therefore ensure that the items under finance that are agreed he shall be concerned with are done properly and that warning signals of anything he sees on the financial front, whether strictly his direct responsibility or not, are passed to his management as it is likely to cause trouble to his project.

It is normal that the actual project management costs of his salary, key management salaries, general expenses and specialised expenses—for example, computer runs for PERT or other management tools—will be prepared and directly controlled by the project manager. The preparation must be in the form of a "bottom up" approach; general estimates have a habit of being undervalued. By building up in the correct manner a much more realistic estimate is assured.

With regard to the total cost of the project this may, in the case of a large civil engineering works, have been built up by several people; the project manager may or may not have been appointed by this time. Some companies appoint only on contract, take the small additional risk of expenditure and get the project manager in at the tender stage if this is practicable. We favour the latter but the former can and does work. While the contract progresses the project manager has to operate with an existing cost framework and the question of overspend or underestimate is sometimes not easy to judge. Checks have to be made by the project manager as the cost returns begin to accumulate and early warning of possible wrong estimating must be given to management as quickly as possible. In setting up the planning the operation of checks and balances on the project manager's budget should be included.

The other main differences in how project finances are operated occur in whether the project is a single entity—a bridge, a hotel, a block of flats, etc—or whether the project is designed to produce a product—for example, a new typewriter, adding machine or television receiver. In the latter case the project manager may have large sums of money under his control, to trade-off money on tooling or plant in order to bring the unit price of the product down. In the single entity project large tooling costs can only be set against the one task and must increase the total price. Whichever use we may be considering, one overriding consideration is to obtain costs from the beginning, and all the time. Well-engineered and novel projects will only sell if the price is right and that means cost control to ensure sufficient profits. The project plan is not a plan without full knowledge of costs.

Many people will not give costs unless they know they are accurate and complete. While these are good motives it is much better to have some idea of costs than no idea at all. Accurate costs too late will not save a company from bankruptcy. We are personally great believers in what we call "filling the cost pot" and we include a similar illustration (Figure 6.2) to that which we had in our previous book on project management (*Successful Project Management*) because the philosophy is so important.

*Materials.* There are two important things to say about materials in general. They sound obvious as with much other management information:

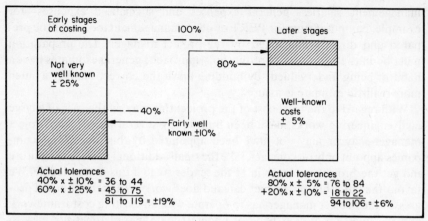

Figure 6.2 THE COST POT

1    In the breakdown of the whole task make sure materials are properly
     identified with task accomplishments except "free issue" materials
     which may not be considered worthwhile to so do. Make sure that the
     plan allows for delivery times—some material takes a long time
2    Materials should be there when required. There is much waste of
     money and labour time on many projects because materials are not
     available at the right time

*Space, services, tools and machinery.* Again the plan must be to have
everything when it is wanted, nothing forgotten, nothing late. A project may
require a particular crane, difficult to obtain because it is heavily booked.
It would not be very profitable to have it or men hanging around because
either of them are mistimed. When it does arrive make sure that all the jobs
it is needed for can be done in the shortest period of time if that is the
economic thing to do. This is where, as will be shown in Chapter 7, the use
of arrow or network diagrams become invaluable. Missing out time-scales,
contractual aspects and progressing (including more about costs) because
they are covered in seperate chapters, we move to a further aspect of planning.

## 6:4 QUALITY AND RELIABILITY

These are items which essentially must be considered from the very start of
a project. No project manager can build reliability into a project where

the items that comprise it are unreliable. If the project is to produce a product selling in quantity the Q & R considerations start from the first moment plans are laid for the product. If the project is a one-off engineering and manufactured item the same thing must be done. If the project is an assembly of pieces then the way those pieces are assembled and used is the second application of Q & R, the first being in the initial engineering and manufacturing of the pieces.

Q & R must be built into the project plan. Quality is not a product made of gold but a product that, if necessary, looks good, is light if it is supposed to be light, small if it has to be small and performs as is should. It is also having a low value of rejects in the factory; and customer satisfaction because the customer sees good value for money.

Reliability is the ability, built in, for the product to continue all the quality aspects for a period of time that was planned. Hopefully this too is long enough, or repairs cheap enough, after this period to keep customer satisfaction and ensure more sales to this customer and others.

The practical task that the project manager can perform is dependent on where the project manager enters the scene. If one can use a computer example of a developed and manufactured product then the development engineering project manager has all the power in his hands consistent with company policy to ensure the right quality and reliability. They cannot be put into the product later, they go in at square one. In fact even before development engineering starts the project definition may have fixed several of the Q & R parameters. The engineering project manager must plan for Q & R. When the computer and all the other items, peripheral equipments, media, etc, are forming an installation the site implementation project manager cannot influence the basic Q & R of the parts. He can, however, help to design the system in such a way that it is not overloaded and that it has changeover ability to standby equipment if necessary, in order to increase the system reliability. Thus system reliability can be affected by the project manager and his work and advice.

## 6:5  VALUE ANALYSIS

This is in a similar category to Q & R. Although the term value analysis springs from a particular application in "value analysing" products made in a American company some twenty years ago the expression turned round is more common place—analysis of value.

Housewives do it every day in their shopping. Husbands do it when they choose a new car. Companies do it when they choose new equipment. Put simply it is:

62

*PRACTICAL PROJECT MANAGEMENT*
1    Getting something for less cost with no reduction in quality or performance
2    Getting something better for less proportionate cost than another item
3    The term "better" can mean performance, reliability, maintainability, appearance or any other factor which the user considers is better

The project manager, in planning the project, should exercise value judgements in all the areas of planning.

## 6:6 SUMMARY OF PLANNING

The type, depth and extent of a project plan is clearly influenced by the industry technicalties, scope and complexity of the project. It depends on how well the route ahead is known or unknown. It depends on customer requirements and contractual commitments. It must include an analysis and understanding of the customer's work. The task must be split into major objectives and subobjectives, each with full definition characteristics. This leads ultimately to the task breakdown in terms of management (who), the jobs (what), the responsibilities (who does what), the time plans (when) and the cost in resources of all types (how much).

## 6:7 SCHEDULING

It may be considered somewhat pedantic to separate planning and scheduling but to distinguish between them helps to emphasise the nature of planning. Plans are translated into schedules by a decision-making process which considers the information in the plan, uses the expected dates and latest allowable dates, utilises any slack routes and assigns resources and facilities. From a practical point of view the plan is the map of the job,the schedule the actual journey accomplishment. In real life there will always be a host of complicating factors that cause the schedule to be a practical realisation of the plan and not a perfect image of the plan. Project competition, availabilty of manpower and facilities and manpower leveling are all real life problems.

Bar charts are one form of practical schedule device provided they are based on a network plan (see section 7:4).

It is clear that the schedule dependence on the plan must remain throughout the project life. The plan will be changed from time to time. Scheduling must result in the practical sense. There are five rough and ready rules to govern the interrelationship:

1    It is the plan that must remain the master item in governing the content and sequence of the work to be done

2    The schedule is the practical operation of the plan. It converts the planned items into acceptable timescales and activities which management can approve

3    The plan must be modified if schedules cannot validate the plan after all effort has been brought to bear

4    The schedule sets the times by which work is started and finished and defines the resources needed for that work

5    In real life, in practical terms, it must be expected that plans and schedules will change. The important thing is to acknowledge this, prepare for it and have a fast method of doing it

# 7

# Timescales

## 7:1 NETWORKS

As part of the early stages of the project definition one should prepare a simple arrow or network diagram commonly known as a macronet showing the significant activities, their timescales and their logical interconnections. It is from this macronet that we shall build the more detailed arrow diagram for the project. Figures 7.1 and 7.3 are simple examples of macronets, although in an actual project generally about 30 to 100 activities would be involved. Each activity has against it the time in weeks or periods chosen (t). We can expand the activities in the macronet as in Figure 7.2

Not all companies or project managers agree about PERT and its various

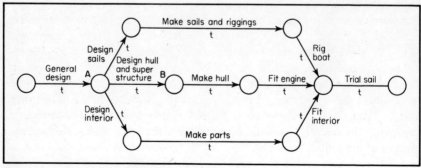

Figure 7.I NEW BOAT NETWORK

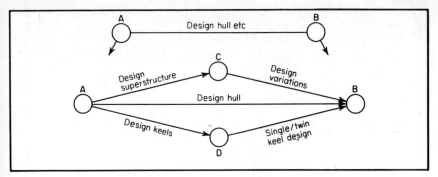

**Figure 7.2** ACTIVITY EXPANSION

advantages and disadvantages and we do not intend to give a full treatise on the subject in this book. [PERT (program evaluation and review technique) was designed to plan and control projects by means of network analysis and has been successfully used in widely differing fields. It is known variously as critical path analysis (CPA) critical path method (monitor) (CPM) and critical path planning (CPP) although the general convention is that PERT includes time, manpower, cost and other resource planning whereas CPA, CPM and CPP usually deal with time only.] However, two things we must say judging from our own experience and that of colleagues in various companies: first, whether PERT is used or not an arrow diagram of a macronet form is essential for early planning; second, we believe that full network planning whether computer run or not has these important advantages over other methods.

1    In the initial preparation of a timeplan for the project and as part of the project plan, the network method forces the mind to think adequately about the logical interrelationships that must properly occur between activities— for example activity 1 must be complete before activity 2 can commence, or activity 1 and 2 must be completed before activity 3 can commence.

2    When the macronet has been expanded and completed into a full network and the content agreed with all parties who supply the resources to actually effect the activities, then the critical or longest time route can be ascertained, with the ascertainment of spare time (or float or slack) on other routes. From this can easily come further efforts towards rationalising or improving the overall timescale by examining the logic, timescales and resources of individual activities.

3    Networks provide a formal planning procedure in the amount of detail required by management.

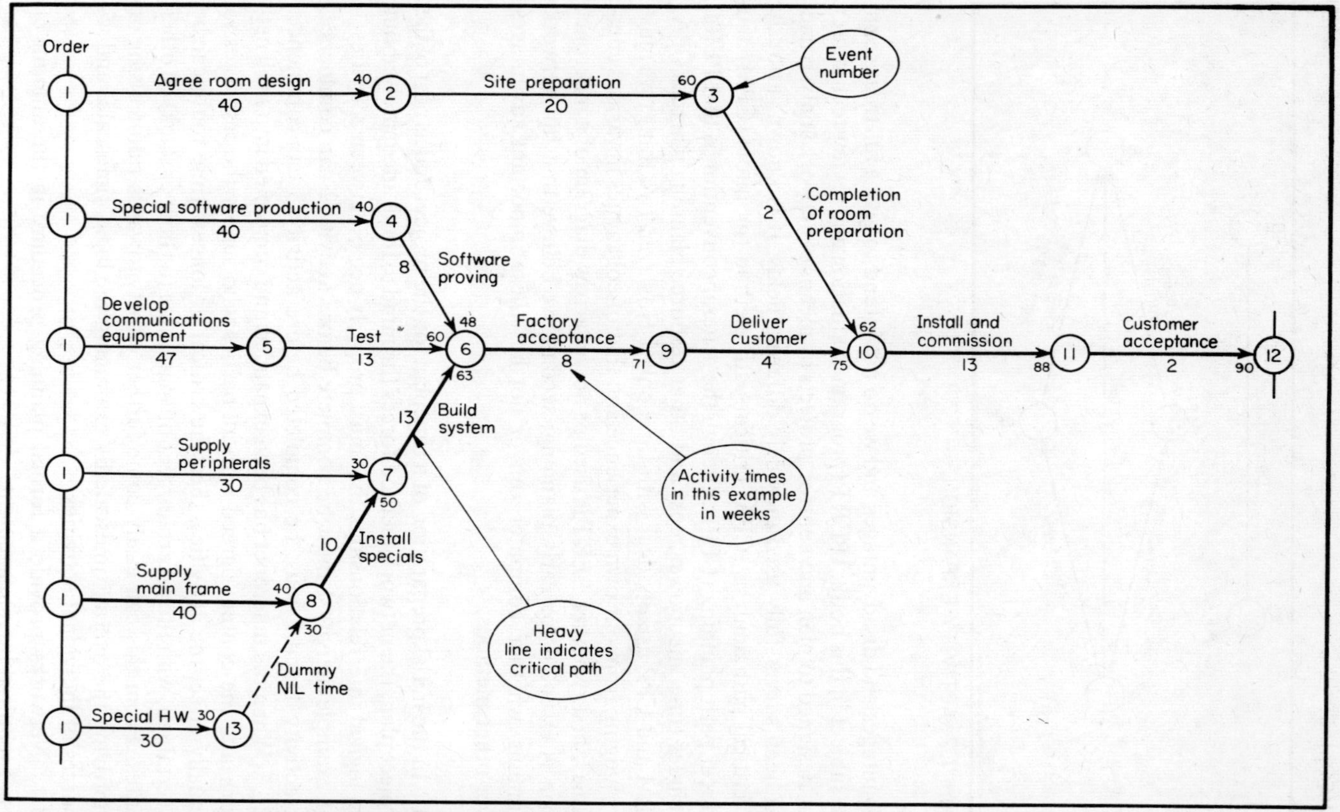

Figure 7.3 SIMPLE COMPUTER PROJECT EXAMPLE

**4** They are an acceptable compromise between over complication and over simplification.

**5** They are good communication documents in that they enable the plan for a project to be seen and discussed clearly.

**6** Networks can be used to simulate the effect of alternative decisions before firm policies are established.

**7** They are flexible in that they can include uncertainties before actual details are known, and they can be updated and reprocessed when errors in estimates become apparent.

**8** Networks can be drawn in detail for those parts of a project that are known; future requirements can be drawn in outline for subsequent enlargement when the facts are known more precisely.

**9** They provide analyses that result in better work schedules being established.

**10** They focus attention on areas that require special notice.

**11** They can be used to monitor progress and highlight possible delays at an early stage so that corrective action can be taken.

**12** They assist the better deployment of resources.

**13** They can be used to calculate and monitor expenditure.

**14** They can be handled by computers. This means that a plan can be documented and reports produced easily and quickly for all levels of management concerned. Any changes in the plan can be communicated with equal facility.

In the progress of the project there will be change. The interaction of any change on the activities can be easily and safely calculated on a network diagram.

Figure 7.2 shows how a single activity on the macronet can be expanded into one or more levels of expansion so that a full network can be produced. It is the case in some project management that the project manager can control the project by a sufficiently detailed macronet because clear interface points at the start and finish of activities can be allied to a particular line management set of activities. In this case the line manager would hold the further levels of the network. The actual procedure obviously depends on what type of project management is being employed.

## 7:2 DATED FORMAT

For management purposes generally, and because most people like to talk in terms of 8 September, 1 November, 20 March, etc, the macronet should

eventually be put either on a dated format or the activities and events on
a dated list as shown in the following example.

| EVENTS | ACTIVITY | DURATION (WEEKS) | BASED ON EARLIEST START | | TOTAL FLOAT (WEEKS) |
|---|---|---|---|---|---|
| | | | START | FINISH | |
| 1 to 2 | Agree room design | 40 | 1 Jan Yr 1 | 7 Oct Yr 1 | 13 |
| 2 to 3 | Site preparation | 20 | 7 Oct Yr 1 | 24 Feb Yr 2 | 13 |
| 3 to 10 | Complete room prep | 2 | 24 Feb Yr 2 | 10 Mar Yr 2 | 13 |
| 1 to 4 | Special software prodn | 40 | 1 Jan Yr 1 | 7 Oct Yr 1 | 15 |
| 4 to 6 | Software proving | 8 | 7 Oct Yr 1 | 2 Dec Yr 1 | 15 |
| 1 to 5 | Dev comms equip | 47 | 1 Jan Yr 1 | 25 Nov Yr 1 | 3 |
| 5 to 6 | Test | 13 | 25 Nov Yr 1 | 24 Feb Yr 2 | 3 |
| 1 to 7 | Supply peripherals | 30 | 1 Jan Yr 1 | 29 July Yr 1 | 20 |
| 1 to 8 | Supply main frame | 40 | 1 Jan Yr 1 | 7 Oct Yr 1 | NIL |
| 8 to 7 | Instal specials | 10 | 7 Oct Yr 1 | 16 Dec Yr 1 | NIL |
| 7 to 6 | Build system | 13 | 16 Dec Yr 1 | 17 Mar Yr 2 | NIL |
| 6 to 9 | Factory acceptance | 8 | 17 Mar Yr 2 | 12 May Yr 2 | NIL |
| 9 to 10 | Delivery to customer | 4 | 12 May Yr 2 | 9 June Yr 2 | NIL |
| 10 to 11 | Instal & commission | 13 | 9 June Yr 2 | 18 Aug Yr 2 | NIL |
| 11 to 12 | Customer acceptance | 2 | 18 Aug Yr 2 | 1 Sept Yr 2 | NIL |
| 1 to 13 | Special hardware | 30 | 1 Jan Yr 1 | 29 July Yr 1 | 10 |
| 13 to 8 | Dummy | NIL | 29 July Yr 1 | 29 July Yr 1 | 10 |

The path through the project from activity 1 to 8 to 7 to 6 to 9 to 10 to 11
and to 12 is called the critical path; there is no time to spare along his route.
In the dated format about it can be seen that in the "total float" (or spare)
column, NIL is entered against the activites on this route. The method of
calculation is simple. Add the times of all activities together until another
activity joins an event. Take the longest time at the event and move on. We
will go through Figure 7.3 without all the activity names to show the
procedure in Figure 7.4.

In the total float column in the dated format table it can be seen, from
looking at event 10 that 13 weeks difference or float or spare time exists in
the route 1 to 2 to 3 to 10 as distinct from the critical path. One can therefore
write on the table in this total float column that 13 weeks total float exists
in each of the activities 1 to 2 or 2 to 3 or 3 to 10. It must be noted that there is
only one lot of 13 weeks—it is total float. If activity 1 to 2 is late by 13 weeks
then activities 2 to 3 and 3 to 10 automatically must be critical—there is no
more float. The other routes are treated in the same way. The bar chart in
Figure 7.5 shows the floats another way.

There are many more complications to the full use of CPM (critical path
monitor) or PERT (program evaluation review technique) but for macronet
work little else really needs to be known. (See the bibliography for recom-
mended reading.)

## 7:3  OTHER USES FOR NETWORKING

Networks can be used in other cases where the term project is not always used. Take the case of plant changeovers and expansions. These might involve for example the addition of new plant to a process plant. A network can show how every piece of new plant is to be assembled into the original, what valves have got to be shut off while this bit is added, what valves to be opened to bring that bit into play and so on.

The flow diagram of the existing process has to be welded into the whole network diagram. The result is a very organised and carefully planned project. Of course there will be problems as in all projects. Perhaps a faulty piece will have to be removed, or a particular section cannot be made available because of a sudden demand for use. Projects are not real without some problems. Overhauls are a very good ground for network planning and by continuously attacking the logic and method of overhaul on the network, much time and money can be saved. Networking is already a proven money saver in such fields as electricity generating station boiler maintenance and overhaul, and process plant maintenance, overhaul and changeover.


## 7:4  BAR CHARTS

Scheduling was mentioned in the last chapter, and bar charts are probably the most popular. What is acceptable and convenient is to bar chart the necessary activities but still retain the key linking as exists in the network.

This is especially useful in macronet working and it is sometimes used as the detail from the macronet instead of fully networking all the details within the project significant activites. Whatever method the project manager eventually uses to detail the macronet is immaterial (quite often this is done by the line management responsible for the activity); it has to be a method that works for the project manager, not some system that he appears to be fighting all the time. We have made clear what we believe to be right and have explained why. The rest is up to the project manager.

Start at the top. The first route without any junction is:

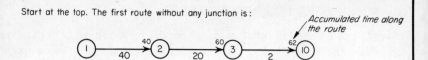

*Accumulated time along the route*

This puts event 10 at 62 weeks via this route. The other routes directly to event 10 cannot be checked because they themselves have junctions but now steadily work down the diagram:

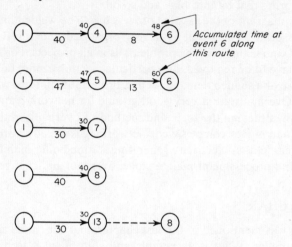

*Accumulated time at event 6 along this route*

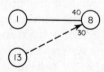

We now continue to move across the network gradually completing the accumulated times; at event 8 the position is now:

Event 8 is shown now to be not capable of being completed until week 40 due to activity 1 to 8. "Carry forward" the 40 weeks up the activity 8 to 7:

*Carried forward*

*Accumulated time due to carry forward from 8 and activity 8 to 7*

Event 7 is:

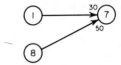

Now carry forward 50 weeks to event 6, that is :

As the figure already at 6 from the route 1 to 5 to 6 is only 60 weeks, therefore it is possible to carry 63 forward to event 9 and, as there is no junction at 9, to event 10:

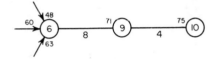

The figure at event 10 (from event 3) was 62 weeks, therefore carry the 75 weeks from above route to 11 and to 12, that is:

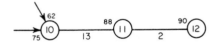

To mark in the critical path it is easiest to come back down the network. The critical path is that directed down the highest carry forward figures, that is :

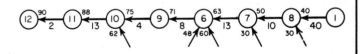

This is the longest or critical path through the network

**Figure 7.4 CRITICAL PATH NETWORKS**

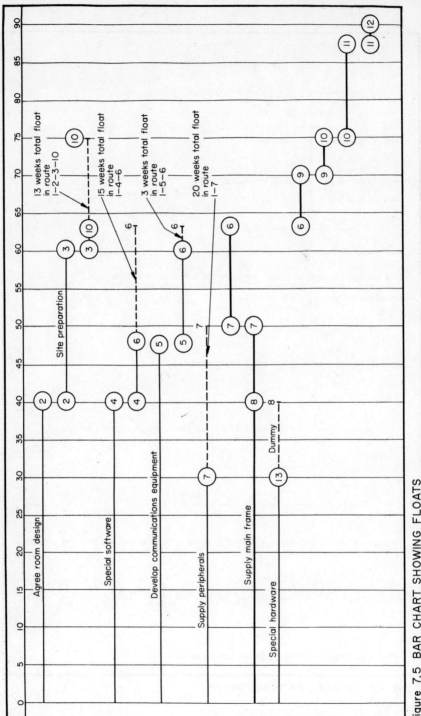

Figure 7.5 BAR CHART SHOWING FLOATS

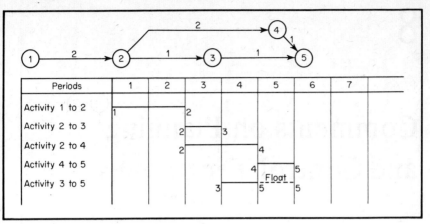

Figure 7.6 BAR CHART, KEY LINKING

# 8

# Comments on Planning and Control Techniques

In all projects the most important aspect is human endeavour, whether of a highly technical nature in a small technical project or a high degree of general management and technical knowledge in a large complex project. There is no substitute for this knowledge; techniques for planning and control must be considered as tools to be used by expert workman. One such tool to receive a great amount of publicity in project work is PERT.

## 8:1 PERT

Many companies use PERT successfully but there is still controversy over its value, especially in the cost and resource aspects. We believe that when used in a commonsense manner it is a highly effective tool. Like all tools, if not used properly it does not do the job expected of it. One of the biggest questions that surrounds its use is how much and what type of PERT data should be reported to progressively higher levels of management. The core of the argument is the conflict that may exist between the line management vertical structure of organisation and information flow as opposed to the project method. In a project there tends to be a more free or open flow of information to satisfy the project concept of lateral and thorough communication. The project has no boundaries other than the project. Another contributory factor is a lack of understanding of the difference between information used for control purposes and that which is generated for assessing progress or establishing objectives.

Lower levels of management do not like the possibility of excessive control, fearing a limitation of their freedom; they try to limit the provision of detailed data. Higher levels of management, anticipating some sort of restriction may try to compensate by asking for more information than they really want, hoping that the result will be at least enough for their requirements. This sort of problem is not unique to PERT situations but exists in all organisations; it is intimately related to much broader considerations of management politics and human behaviour.

Companies have their own unique solutions. We have written earlier about the importance of giving at all times the truth to higher management but we appreciate that, for example, the giving of anticipated slippage dates can cause problems. It is up to management to recognise that if they expect lower levels of management to act responsibly so must they. If a subordinate gets into trouble every time he tells the truth because he wants to play his proper part then he will soon stop and the project will suffer. Use of PERT makes any deception difficult so that unpleasant and perhaps critical situations will develop without enlightened management reaction. Subordinate managers of course may fall into the trap of not reporting latenesses because of the hope that all will be well in the end.

There may be no need for concern but any slippage is serious because of possible snowballing effects. Higher management therefore have a duty to see that an education process exists to show how trade-offs and alternate approaches may be employed to leave the same amount of safety in the plan. The sequences as shown in a PERT network may have to be changed to recover the full position. A manager is rarely constrained to a single sequence of activities in accomplishing a task. Alternatives may not of necessity increase cost or technical risk. Lower levels of management may also not be in possession of the best solution in the broad interest of the project. Higher management have more options open to them because of their intrinsically wider perspective. These points direct to the vital need for full and free flows of information in and around the project and to the various levels of management. This, PERT can help to provide. In order to avoid some of the common problems of management reporting that we mention above, a PERT system should allow for the following concepts:

1    Careful breakdown of responsibilities with full identification and accountability for each work package
2    Schedules should show clearly the interrelationships between the work and various levels of management control
3    Accomplishment "milestones" used for control purposes should be distinguished from general information. This will prevent any inhibi-

tion of free information flow while enabling responsibility to remain on the milestone path
4    There should be a clear difference between current assessments of expected completion dates, planned dates, and various calculated dates of other types

How these concepts are applied in a particular project is up to the management concerned and is peculiar to an industry. What we often do as a practical case is to structure the total task by levels of responsibility, two or three being usually adequate. Each level has its own milestones and is free to work to achieve its milestones provided that the execution of the work is within the technical, resource and schedule limits established for that level.

In looking further at PERT it should be recognised that the final answer, as in so many management tools, is only as good as the basic information that went into building up the network, and later updating it. Some further comments on the practical use of PERT are:

1    PERT is deceptively simple. Real life presents many problems. It is essential not to get too much detail in the first look at the network and only to increase the level of detail to that required to retain control. It is only too easy to make a PERT network so cumbersome that it cannot be understood by anybody. It then loses credence which is unfortunate as its use is probably badly needed. If the task is a very large one the network may well be able to be split down into several parts provided that the interfaces between the networks can be thoroughly identified and that there is no loss of logical lock between the networks.

2    It may not be the right thing to use PERT beyond the early stages of a project. It is highly effective at the start; of that there is little argument in project management circles, significant benefits being obtained. Later on it may demand too much attention for the return it gives and some other method of control may be appropriate.

3    Unless the management of a company is determined to get full value from PERT it is easy for it to be used in a half-hearted and ineffective manner. PERT clashes with traditional organisational patterns. It is a tool that knows no boundaries and if allowed to will soon bring into the open any nonperformers. This is not liked by people who are used to great freedom in their functional span of control. There are of course the innumerable arguments about line management and its responsibilities. Because of this the full potential of the system for integrating the entire project effort including an overall analysis of schedule, resource and technical performance data is often not realised.

**4** Intellectual management involvement is essential by the project manager, staff and higher management. If this cannot be so it might be better not to use PERT as the apparent benefit would be less than hoped for involving disappointment and confusion. However the risk that a project runs without the logical approach of PERT or CPA, etc, to aid it means that managment should try to give this intellectual involvement. No company these days works without some budgeting and accounting control system. Similarly no project should be operated without learning how to use effective management tools.

If it is decided for good reasons that the full use of PERT is likely to prove too complex for the company concerned then at least CPA (or CPM or CPP whichever name you prefer) should be used. A determination to succeed is obviously required and the reward is a much clearer and safer project plan. Many companies ironically have suffered from too great a determination in persisting with PERT, CPA, etc, too long when other progressing methods may be more appropriate especially at later stages in the project. In projects where the later stage is an output of a product in quantity the line of balance technique may be better.

## 8:2   LINE OF BALANCE (LOB)

As with other progressing methods the object is first to plan, second to be able to monitor the plan, and finally to derive corrective actions from the monitoring. LOB enables this to be done and a simple example will make the method clear. How it is used after that depends very much on the application and the whim of the progresser. There are two main requirements: an output of quantities at predetermined intervals and a process or production cycle.

*Output.*   This is most easily represented by a table of output quantities against say, weeks (see Figure 8.1).

*Production cycle.*   There are two parts to this, the flow diagram of work and the part quantities. An example of the principal parts for an item could look like Figure 8.2.

The planning problem is to find out what quantities of assemblies *A, B, C* and *D*, with fitting and test time are required week by week to meet the output as in Figure 8.3. In week 1 we know we want 200 completed items including test. To achieve this we also know we want 200 tested items two weeks before. The assemblies must be ready before that. By using the output table and the production cycle information a completed picture of the assembly requirements prior to an output date can be derived (Figure 8.4).

| Week number | Weekly output | Cumulative output | Week number | Weekly output | Cumulative output |
|---|---|---|---|---|---|
| 1 | 200 | 200 | 8 | 250 | 1635 |
| 2 | 150 | 350 | 9 | 250 | 1885 |
| 3 | 300 | 650 | 10 | 210 | 2095 |
| 4 | 200 | 850 | 11 | 260 | 2355 |
| 5 | 175 | 1025 | 12 | 280 | 2635 |
| 6 | 160 | 1185 | 13 | 240 | 2875 |
| 7 | 200 | 1385 | 14 | 200 | 3075 |

Figure 8.1 OUTPUT QUANTITIES FOR LINE OF BALANCE

One can plot the results in a form of a graph as the objectives for the output. This can be combined with a progress chart alongside the graph. However, it should be remembered that all these sorts of planning and progressing aids are tools, or, perhaps better expressed as ideas; they can be dressed up in many ways as the progresser desires, provided the essential aim is realised, to help plan and progress accurately and swiftly.

When the graph and progress chart are complete one can mark off any shortages represented on the progress chart by hatched areas below the line of balance. One can then lay-off the shortages on the objectives graph to see the full effect. Assembly *A* sets completion has a shortfall back to 2800. This will not affect the output in week 4 but will, if not put right, limit total production (or make the final output late). As assembly *A* sets is a 10 week item—that is 10 weeks lead time—one can mark in 2800 at 14 weeks (10 weeks lead + review week 4). Similarly the shortfall in *A* sets will ripple down through the sequence unless something is done—that is, assembly *A* sets

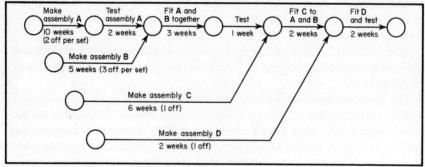

Figure 8.2 PRODUCT MAIN ASSEMBLY NETWORK

| Week | Items ready for test | | Assembly D (one off) completed | | Assembly C (one off) completed | | A and B ready for test | | Assembly A tested | | Assembly B completed (3 off per set) | | Assembly A completed (2 off per set) | |
|---|---|---|---|---|---|---|---|---|---|---|---|---|---|---|
| | Per week | Cum | Per week | Cum | Per week | Cum | Per week | Cum | Per week | Cum | Per week | Cum | Per week | Cum |
| −14 | | | | | | | | | | | | | | |
| −13 | | | | | | | | | | | | | | |
| −12 | | | | | | | | | | | | | | |
| −11 | | | | | | | | | | | | | | |
| −10 | | | | | | | | | | | | | 200 | 200 |
| −9 | | | | | | | | | | | | | 150 | 350 |
| −8 | | | | | | | | | 200 | 200 | 200 | 200 | 300 | 650 |
| −7 | | | | | | | | | 150 | 350 | 150 | 350 | 200 | 850 |
| −6 | | | | | | | | | 300 | 650 | 300 | 650 | 175 | 1025 |
| −5 | | | | | | | 200 | 200 | 200 | 850 | 200 | 850 | 160 | 1185 |
| −4 | | | | | 200 | 200 | 150 | 350 | 175 | 1025 | 175 | 1025 | 200 | 1385 |
| −3 | | | | | 150 | 350 | 300 | 650 | 160 | 1185 | 160 | 1185 | 250 | 1635 |
| −2 | 200 | 200 | 200 | 200 | 300 | 650 | 200 | 850 | 200 | 1385 | 200 | 1385 | 250 | 1885 |
| −1 | 150 | 350 | 150 | 350 | 200 | 850 | 175 | 1025 | 250 | 1635 | 250 | 1635 | 210 | 2095 |
| 1 | 300 | 650 | 300 | 650 | 175 | 1025 | 160 | 1185 | 250 | 1885 | 250 | 1885 | 260 | 2355 |
| 2 | 200 | 850 | 200 | 850 | 160 | 1185 | 200 | 1385 | 210 | 2095 | 210 | 2095 | 280 | 2635 |
| 3 | 175 | 1025 | 175 | 1025 | 200 | 1385 | 250 | 1635 | 260 | 2355 | 260 | 2355 | 240 | 2875 |
| 4 | 160 | 1185 | 160 | 1185 | 250 | 1635 | 250 | 1885 | 280 | 2635 | 280 | 2635 | 200 | 3075 |
| 5 | 200 | 1385 | 200 | 1385 | 250 | 1885 | 210 | 2095 | 240 | 2875 | 240 | 2875 | | |
| 6 | 250 | 1635 | 250 | 1635 | 210 | 2095 | 260 | 2355 | 200 | 3075 | 200 | 3075 | | |
| 7 | 250 | 1885 | 250 | 1885 | 260 | 2355 | 280 | 2635 | | | | | | |
| 8 | 210 | 2095 | 210 | 2095 | 280 | 2635 | 240 | 2875 | | | | | | |
| 9 | 260 | 2355 | 260 | 2355 | 240 | 2875 | 200 | 3075 | | | | | | |
| 10 | 280 | 2635 | 280 | 2635 | 200 | 3075 | | | | | | | | |
| 11 | 240 | 2875 | 240 | 2875 | | | | | | | | | | |
| 12 | 200 | 3075 | 200 | 3075 | | | | | | | | | | |
| 13 | | | | | | | | | | | | | | |
| 14 | | | | | | | | | | | | | | |

Figure 8.3 TABLE OF ASSEMBLY REQUIREMENTS

tested will be 175 short (3075–2900); *A* and *B* ready for test and items ready
for test. Each of these can be lined across to the appropriate week and a new
graph point fixed. Assembly *A* tested has an 8 week lead time, hence review
week 4 + 8 = 12 weeks line. Assembly *A* and *B* ready for test has five week
lead time, hence review week 4 + 5 = 9 week line.

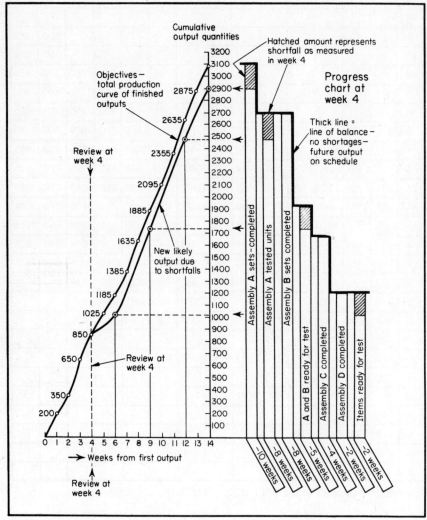

Figure 8.4   LINE OF BALANCE OBJECTIVES AND PROGRESS CHART

## 8:3  BAR CHARTS

Undoubtedly these are the most used of all simple planning and control techniques. Examples are shown in Chapter 7, whereby the dependencies of one activity are shown by numbering the connections with the same activity. This soon gets tedious if a chain of changes occurs and it can involve much redrawing without the same certainty as in a network diagram that the logic will still be right. However, for a great deal of scheduling work the bar chart has few equals. There have been several attempts to marry up the bar chart with networking but we personally have not yet seen anything satisfactory.

# 9

# Project Progressing

All project managers are faced with the problem that any manager has—the need to avoid trivialities and to concentrate on essentials. One essential action for a project manager is to take sufficient time to regularly check the project progress. It is all too easy to become absorbed in a part of the whole task and forget the ultimate goal. Without time to thoroughly check the project progress there may be no more time. The project may fail.

Like many tasks, progressing can be made much easier if standard procedures are adopted. These do not usurp a project manager's management and technical skills but provide virtual checklists for progressing and a view of the project progress for management. No project manager could or should content himself with only a mechanistic approach, such as a check-list, but the usefulness of standard procedures should not be underestimated. In this day and age, management cannot be satisfied by the project manager who says: "Don't worry, things are all right." There must be a measure of justification. Checklists and reporting methods can provide a convenient vehicle for some of this.

In practical terms any project has four criteria by which its progress can be measured. These are:

1    Timescales and individual activity progress
2    Costs and other resources
3    Performance
4    The relationship between those three at any one time

## 9:1   TIMESCALES

A network of all the activities that make up the project is essential in order to control it properly. From this network the more familiar bar charts for local progressing and management reporting can be derived. The network does not necessarily have to be very large. It is much more important that it provides for:

1   All significant activites
2   Well-considered and sensible activity times
3   A practical logic
4   A means for understanding and progressing the project

Many people think that a network has to be progressed on a computer. This is not necessarily so. It entirely depends on the number of activities; when one gets above 250 activities progressing by hand becomes tedious and computer up-dating is probably desirable. It is relatively cheap as it is a standard procedure in these days. Whether by computer or not, however, the main task of the project manager is not a mechanical one. He must be concerned to look at the main issues on the timescale in an intensely practical manner. He must bear in mind the fact that:

**1**   The critical path will change from time to time in a normal project. One that keeps precisely according to plan may indeed be suspect in some way. It may mean that the plan is really inadequate. One should not be lulled into complacency and should re-examine all activities and longer-term implications. Obviously this applies to complex projects. In a very simple one the critical path may indeed remain the same.

**2**   There must be a continuous examination of the logic of the situation and with the plan automatically and regularly reviewed the project manager has the opportunity to value analyse it at each up-dating session. Just because a plan was drawn out in the first place does not mean that it cannot be changed. If it looks right to change it as the project proceeds then it should be changed. The project is a live dynamic thing and must be treated accordingly. One of the dangers that must be watched for is any tendency to look at an unfinished activity and believe that it will be all right in the end and therefore proceed happily to the next task. It is like building on uncertain foundations. The judgement on whether certain activities are complete is a difficult and professional task and must be treated accordingly.

**3**   Allied to the activities progress will be the question of resources. These are dealt with under the heading of "costs and resources" in the next section.

It is important to realise that all areas of progress are very much interrelated and the project manager must be constantly aware of this fact, otherwise there is a danger of achievement in one area only.

*Timescales and people.*   Two problems that affect timescales a great deal are concerned with the way people react to estimating and to things going wrong. Many people are optimistic and even if an activity is running late they will persist in saying it will be all right on the day. The day comes and they then say, well it will be another week and so it goes on. Even skilled and intelligent people fall into this trap. It is something akin to pride and an almost hypnotic belief that it must come out all right. This is where progressing has to be carried out to a degree which borders on interference because all progress is made up of little bits of progress. According to the confidence the project manager has in a reporting source so he progresses larger or smaller chunks. In the end the project manager is responsible and must protect the project's interest.

Another problem bound up with the first is the question of not asking for help. Many people feel it is an admission of defeat to ask for help or to report a situation that is going wrong. They think they should be able to deal with the situation. What they do not realise is that some problems really cannot be solved by them alone—more help and resources are needed and someone else can master it but not they. This problem is one of pride and the project manager must be on his guard.

No one should feel that in these cases the people are entirely inadequate and should be replaced. If they are satisfactory in other respects the project manager must educate them by showing them the danger to the project of either progressing fault. He must also not fall into the same trap himself.

*The progressing cycle.*   The general timescale preparation and progressing activity is shown in Figure 9.1.

Although the diagram appears to lay emphasis on plan preparation the key question included in the cycle is: "is the current plan satisfactory?" From this the periodic status reports are derived. If the current plan is not satisfactory, actions as indicated must be carried out.

*Trade-offs.*   As with all the progressing activities the project manager will be continually faced with the need to make trade-off decisions. They may be simple ones such as: "it is better to get on with some particular task outside because it is fine than commit labour on an inside task." More often the trade-offs will be more complex. To save time on a job on or near the critical path may cost more money. The decision is not only whether to spend, but

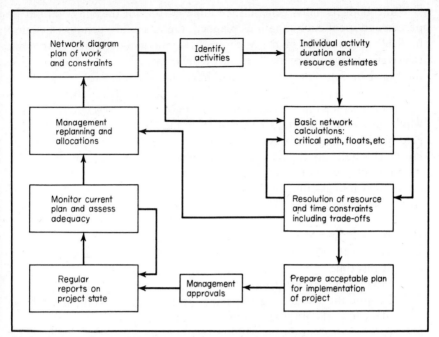

Figure 9.I GENERAL PREPARATION AND PROGRESSING FLOW CHART

how much to spend. A job may look in danger from a subcontractor. It appears it can be done elsewhere for more money. What decision shall be made? What are the contract implications? Will there be cancellation charges? Performance of an engineering product may be below specification—how long will it take, how long can it take and how much for different times to get it right?

Trade-offs are not just last-ditch decisions. Sometimes it is of considerable advantage to deliberately seek for trade-offs. Value analysis and value engineering are forms of trade-off procedures.

## 9:2 COSTS AND RESOURCES

There will be a budget for the project task in terms of money and other resources, including that of manpower. Methods must be adopted to carefully control and monitor the use of these resources against the budget, although the project manager must always be ready to trade-off any one of these against any other factor in the project task. Again, no plan is unassailable and the project manager must always be ready to change his resource allocation around to meet the project need.

While budgets must generally be adhered to, not only in total but in percentage spent each month as planned, the adage of "pennywise pound foolish" can be true in many cases. It is not inconceivable that some relatively inexpensive activity can lie on the critical path. Its price may have increased or a problem with it may have doubled its price. If a project manager effects too much economy and causes the item to be late because he insists on keeping the activity cost down, he is running a grave risk that the whole project may be late. A half-million pound project late for a week could give rise to many hundreds of pounds in interest charges if patment is delayed. This quite apart from other overrun costs and possibly penalties. The moral is not to economise on critical-path items of relatively small value. It is always useful to ask oneself simple practical questions in a control situation. In examining costs one can ask the following:

1    What is the project cost to date?
2    What is the relationship between this actual cost and the planned cost at this time?
3    What is the project progress to date?
4    How do the actual costs of specific accomplishments compare with the planned costs of these accomplishments?
5    Is the project now expected to overrun or underrun the total planned costs?
6    How do all the above questions apply to individual activities and groups of activities in the whole project?

These are searching questions that have to be answered in order to examine, evaluate and control the project costs.

On many projects, apart from risks of overrun, the project manager may find that cost control is fairly easy. He may have a team of people implementing items with fixed prices. The "people" charge will not vary unduly from that planned, although there may be continuing battles over "extras."

On projects where flows of materials and labour are large the necessity for control increases, and inevitably the project manager will have access to skilled financial assistance to ensure control. On civil and building work the weather conditions, materials, and labour availability can play havoc with expenditure and the situation is constantly under review. In practical terms two things are happening. The project/site manager will ensure that all materials and labour are logged onto site. This is costed by the costing office and immediate returns supplied to the project manager. He must be able, by his detailed progressing systems, to make judgement on whether he is keeeping to budget. He must be able to justify both over- and underspend in any period and produce trend reports to show management that the job is under control. There are many cost control systems but all involve basic logging and returns of costs information. The biggest problem, and one seldom tackled adequately, is the measurment in money terms of actual progress itself relative to the whole. What has been spent is easy to calculate. What has been done is not so easy to assess.

What is the project cost to date? This was the first of the questions. The answer should not be difficult to provide as it is a logging process and in its simplest form the answer is a series of expenditure additions. There may be some complications with committed expenditure not yet actually paid. These are considered as well in logging the costs and the result is a table similar to the following. To answer the second question at the same time (what is the relationship with planned costs?) the planned cost figures are written in at the left.

| WEEK (OR PERIOD) | PLANNED COST | ACTUAL COST (PAID OR RECORDED) | COMMITTED COST EXTRA TO ACTUAL |
|---|---|---|---|
| 1 | 1000 | 800 | 200 |
| 2 | 1300 | 1200 | 500 |
| 3 | 1200 | 1200 | 300 |
| 4 | 1500 | 1500 | 500 |

It is then better to add in cumulative figures as well so that a running control total can be easily seen.

| WEEK (OR PERIOD) | PLANNED COST | | ACTUAL COST | | COMMITTED COST EXTRA TO ACTUAL | | ACTUAL PLUS COMMITMENTS |
|---|---|---|---|---|---|---|---|
| | PERIOD | CUM | PERIOD | CUM | PERIOD | CUM | CUM |
| | £ | £ | £ | £ | £ | £ | £ |
| 1 | 1000 | 1000 | 800 | 800 | 200 | 200 | 1000 |
| 2 | 1300 | 2300 | 1200 | 2000 | 500 | 700 | 2700 |
| 3 | 1200 | 3500 | 1200 | 3200 | 800 | 1500 | 4700 |
| 4 | 1500 | 5000 | 1500 | 4700 | 500 | 2000 | 6700 |

The commitments can cause confusion either way. We prefer to add them to the record of invoices paid or transfer effected in the accounting system because they are going to show up later and in the meantime perhaps hide a resource problem. When they are paid or recorded in the accounting system the "actual" figure goes up as in the fourth week above and the committal figure goes down to the period commital only. Truth must out all the time and money committed is to all intents and purposes money spent. However, the accounting returns will normally show actuals and hence the committals procedure.

What is the project progress to date? This is an important corollary to any cost information because with costs precisely on target the project could be running late and the final cost therefore be greater. Bound up with this question is the next—actual cost versus planned costs, of specific accomplishments. The second question is important because it is from this examination of parts of the project costs and progress that one can properly relate real progress on the cost time and performance front.

Managers of large-scale projects often find this relationship difficult to define clearly and accurately, either for themselves or for corporate management. It is not uncommon for the accounting department to sharply remind the project manager that he is exceeding his budget while the operations management are congratulating themselves, and perhaps the project manager, that the project is ahead of schedule.

The essentials of good cost/progress reporting are:

1   Costs and accomplishments must be displayed or recorded at the same time
2   Predictions of the cost to complete must be available
3   The system must not be too complicated or expensive to run
4   It must not interfere with intermediate progress reporting which must still be meaningful without the cost information
5   It must provide reports that are easily understood by all levels of management

It is possible to use as the basis for the cost/progress reporting first the cumulative cost figures from the table already shown, thus:

| WEEK | CUMULATIVE COST | |
|---|---|---|
|  | BUDGET | ACTUAL |
|  | £ | £ |
| 1 | 1000 | 1000 |
| 2 | 2300 | 2700 |
| 3 | 3500 | 4700 |
| 4 | 5000 | 6700 |

The next step is to relate the physical accomplishments to accomplishments in terms of budgeted costs. To simply relate physical accomplishment to timescales does not make clear whether overspend or underspend is significant when measured against time progress. Like most sensible and practical methods the cost accomplishment method requires planning from the start. It is necessary to set out in the planning to show that if a key event is reached and satisfactorily passed, it clearly means that a certain proportion of the planned costs have been incurred relative to progress.

Once these cost progress packages have been defined then we add another set of figures which are the cumulative value of work done.

| WEEK (OR PERIOD) | CUMULATIVE COST BUDGET | ACTUAL | CUMULATIVE VALUE OF WORK DONE |
|---|---|---|---|
| | £ | £ | £ |
| 1 | 1000 | 1000 | 1000 |
| 2 | 2300 | 2700 | 3000 |
| 3 | 3500 | 4700 | 4500 |
| 4 | 5000 | 6700 | 7000 |

This immediately shows that although week 4 (or period 4) is overspent in terms of cash the value of work done is well ahead of budget and just a little better than the actual cost.

## 9:3   PREPARATION

From the start of planning a project remember that one of the requirements of the plan is that it should be capable of being progressed in due course. The smaller the unit of work accomplishment that can be valued the more accurate the cost/progress reporting, but to go down to very small amounts makes the process lengthy, cumbersome and unnecessarily expensive. The usual way is to take a unit related to the cost of the job. If the job is a £5000 one then units of £500 for the value of accomplishment may be suitable. If the job is £250 000 then units of £5000 may be considered appropriate. It depends very much on the type of work, how far it is possible to go off course, and how fast one can go off course. A simple example will illustrate the method.

COST BUILD UP OF A SMALL BUILDING
ON A CONCRETE BASE

| | |
|---|---|
| Cement | £  50 |
| Sand | 50 |
| Ballast | 20 |
| Bricks | 500 |
| Doors and windows | 100 |
| Roof materials | 100 |
| Labour | 300 |
| Sundries | 50 |
| | £1170 |

THE JOB IS ESTIMATED TO TAKE 5 WEEKS

In progressing a task like this it is easy to log the expenditure and fairly easy to form an estimate of how the timescale is proceeding. What is difficult is to relate the two. Instead of laying out the costs as above, divide up the complete job into sensible blocks of work on a practical basis as below:

COST BUILD UP IN ORDER TO PROGRESS THE JOB

**1  Preparation of footings**

|                |        |
|----------------|--------|
| Labour         | £  45  |
| Cement         | 10     |
| Sand           | 3      |
| Ballast        | 20     |

| 1st week |            |
|----------|------------|
| EACH     | CUMULATIVE |
| £  78    | £  78      |

**2  Build walls ready to receive door and windows**

|                |        |
|----------------|--------|
| Labour         | £  45  |
| Bricks         | 100    |
| Cement         | 10     |
| Sand           | 13     |

| 2nd week |        |
|----------|--------|
| £168     | £246   |

**3  Fit doors and windows**

|                    |        |
|--------------------|--------|
| Doors and windows  | £100   |
| Sundries           | 30     |
| Labour             | 35     |

| $\frac{1}{2}$ of 3rd week |            |
|---------------------------|------------|
| EACH                      | CUMULATIVE |
| £165                      | £411       |

**4  Complete walls to window Height**

|                |        |
|----------------|--------|
| Bricks         | £250   |
| Labour         | 60     |
| Cement         | 15     |
| Sand           | 16     |

$\frac{1}{2}$ of 3rd week & $\frac{1}{2}$ of 4th week

| £341 | £752 |
|------|------|

**5  Complete walls**

|                |        |
|----------------|--------|
| Bricks         | £150   |
| Labour         | 65     |
| Cement         | 15     |
| Sand           | 18     |

$\frac{1}{2}$ of 4th week

| £248 | £1000 |
|------|-------|

**6  Fit roof**

|                 |        |
|-----------------|--------|
| Roof materials  | £100   |
| Sundries        | 20     |
| Labour          | 50     |

| 5th week |        |
|----------|--------|
| £170     | £1170  |

£1170

From this breakdown into accomplishments a simple cost/time/accomplishment chart can be prepared (Figure 9.2). (The budget line only is shown.) The important difference between this chart and a normal cost/time chart is that right from the start one is plotting items in accomplishment packages.

If at the end of the first week the footings are complete but £100 has

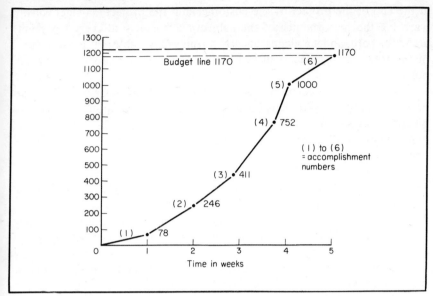

Figure 9.2 ACCOMPLISHMENT COST CHART

been spent (some of this may be an estimate of materials used e.g. sand and cement), one knows immediately that the accomplishment value is £78 and that one has incurred a real overspend of £22 relative to the accomplishment. If all one knew was that the total cost of the building was £1170, even though one knew exactly what materials and labour made up that £1170, one should not be able to judge the cost/progress of the accomplishments correctly.

Multiply the simple job illustrated by tens and hundreds and the problem becomes acute unless it is known how to measure the cost against time accomplishment as above.

It is necessary to have sufficient records to enable one to monitor the situation, make judgements and then decisions to control the situation.

This means that cost knowledge and control starts right at the very onset of the project, the tender stage. Bulk costs without breakdowns for cost progressing will not enable sensible project progressing to be carried out.


9:4 PERFORMANCE

In Chapter 1 the need to define the task that has to be achieved was stressed. The measurement of the achievement is usually by some test or examination at the end of the project by the customer, but the project manager will be watching the performance of the subject achievement at every key point along the path, and it is clear that early warning of possible non-achievement of the total performance can be obtained if proper monitoring is carried out.

A project completed on time, at the budgeted cost, but which does not perform the function the customer and supplier agreed upon is not a completed project at all.

It is important that the project manager takes three positive steps in connection with performance. He should:

1    Make sure that no possible ambiguity exists in the customer's mind and his own company's mind regarding the performance of the project
2    Make sure that adequate tests are devised to show the customer that the performance criteria have been met and obtain the customer's agreement in writing
3    Plan intermediate performance targets so that the project can be measured "along the road"

Only then can the project manager claim a successful performance "end" to the project. (There may be other criteria such as maintenance and serviceability.)

It will be clear from the section just concluded on costs that accomplishments, broken down in the way described, could apply equally well in a more complex situation where performance as well as completion is measured at various stages of completion. For example, in an engineering project there will probably be several tests on unit items prior to their being assembled into a complete unit. Overall performance parameters may well be drawn from these unit tests, although it is certain that only an overall test will fully check the overall performance.

In some projects, such as building a bridge, it is not very feasible to have a halfway test. However, items for the construction will have either standard test results available or similar items specially tested so that the overall "performance," in this case carrying capacity, life and serviceability can be properly gauged.

## 9:5  RELATIONSHIP BETWEEN TIMESCALES, COST AND PERFORMANCE

We hope it is clear from what we have said that cost is indivisible from progress. While in the simple example the matter of performance was not really in question it would obviously be so in many other cases. An accomplishment which was apparently complete but which had a below par performance would not be complete. The three progressing items are in reality but one and no project manager can think of one without the other.

## 9:6 SUMMARY

A progressing system must ensure:

1    That it can effectively measure progress against cost, time and performance parameters and objectives
2    That output of the right kind from this progressing is available to provide different levels of management with the information needed for decision making
3    That it enables all levels of management, particularly the project manager, to define and assess priorities in the task of meeting objectives

Practical project managers know that ideal control systems do not exist. They do, however, know that to try always for an ideal control system will bring them much nearer to it. Sloppy management born of scorn for the

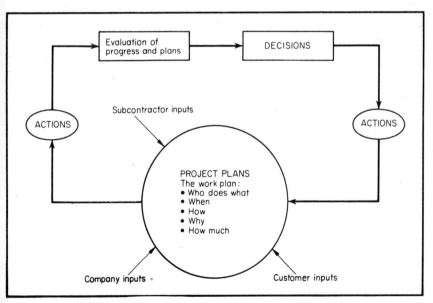

Figure 9.3 PROGRESSING CYCLE

seeker after ideals is dangerous. It is vital to have an organised approach
to project progressing and control. This means that an understandable control framework must exist so that as far as possible major problems can be
anticipated and deviations from the plan corrected.

# 10

# Change Control

From our own experience and from all we have learnt from other projects, we are convinced that one of the critical factors in deciding success or failure of a project is change control. It is generally accepted that a clear project definition is required so that all concerned know precisely what is to be done. It is sometimes overlooked that in a complex project, the execution of which stretches over an appreciable period, there are bound to be changes to the project definition.

These changes may arise for a whole range of reasons. At the simplest the original project definition may contain straight errors of drafting or typing and may need amendment to correct them. The sense may be obscure or ambiguous and need clarification. There may be a clash or conflict between two or more sections of the project definition, which makes them inconsistent. Most systems evolve over the course of time. There may be cases where those who are doing the work on the project may see the possibility of considerable economy or improvement in performance if a certain change can be made to the project definition. They may equally find it very difficult or even impossible to meet the project definition unless it is changed.

Technical advances may make a change desireable. Perhaps most important of all, the user may simply change his mind as to his requirements. No project goes ahead in a vacuum, change is going on all around and it is bound to have some effect on the user's requirements and on the way the project is executed. The law may be changed in such a way as to alter the user requirements. For instance, change in the laws relating to safety and environmental pollution may well have to be reflected in changes to the project definition.

## 10:1  ESSENTIALS OF A CHANGE CONTROL PROCEDURE

If it is accepted that change is invevitable, then one should be prepared for it. Any project plan should include a procedure for establishing and agreeing a project definition, which provides a reference baseline for the project. It must also include a procedure for changing the baseline.

The change control procedure normally operates from the point at which an agreed baseline exists. This baseline should be committed to paper and identical copies of the baseline should be held by all the main participants to the project. Main participants because the project definition baseline is likely to be a fairly bulky document and a lot of work will be involved in keeping it up to date and in operating the change control procedures. There is therefore little point in providing a copy of the complete baseline to a small subcontractor responsible for providing some fairly small well defined item—for example, the supply of air-conditioning chiller units or the supply of computer terminal security badges. However, for such participants who do not receive the baseline document, there must be someone—either in the project team or a main contractor—responsible for ensuring that the effect of change on the minor participant is evaluated.

Change control procedures are likely to vary in detail from industry to industry, but the essential requirements of any such procedure are:

1   All those who may be affected by a proposed change must be consulted
2   Details of the proposed change and all information relevant to the change must be made available to those evaluating it
3   The full impact of a proposed change on work already completed or in hand, on future work and on the operation and maintenance phases of the project must be identified and details made available to those evaluating the proposed change
4   A system which provides a clear record of the progress of all proposed changes and of the final decision on them. It should also be such that no proposed changes become lost in the system
5   The ability to progress some proposed changes at high speed while progressing all changes with a reasonable degree of promptitude
6   A formal procedure for the review of all proposed changes, once they have been evaluated, by a decision making body

7   A system for the control and issue of amendments to the project definition baseline, resulting from the approval of a proposed change

Those concerned only with projects executed in house within large organisations may think that this is an unnecessary elaboration, which will merely cause delay and expense. We do not agree. The need for change control may be more obvious in a customer/contractor situation but the need for tight control exists in all project situations. It is true that in devising your own change control procedure, you will have to reconcile two important conflicting demands: first is the absolute need for tight control of change in order to keep "contractual" relationships between user and project team straight and to keep control over project timescales, cost and performance; second is the need to recognise that the project does not stand still while a proposed change is evaluated. There may be times when delay in agreeing to implement a proposed change results in unnecessary work being done which has later to be undone, thus increasing the cost of the project and leading to delay in completion of it. Notwithstanding this second demand one absolute project rule must be that all parties work to the approved project definition base line until formal approval is given to a change.

## 10:2   CHANGE CONTROL PROCEDURES

The change control procedure outlined below has been simplified but is typical of the procedures used on large and complex computer projects. We lay no claim to originality. Any professionally managed project of this sort is likely to have a similar system. We have preferred to outline a system with which we are familiar rather than a theoretical system which would hopefully be of more general applicability. We have done this because we believe it is better to outline a system which works in a particular set of circumstances. Readers can then compare this with the conditions that exist in their own industry.

The circumstances in which this particular change control procedure are operated are when a customer places a contract with a supplier for computer equipment and associated programs to do the work connected with a particular system. The customer is represented by a project manager, but behind him lie a number of user departments, even including outside concerns that have the final say on the user requirements.

The user requirements are enshrined in a detailed user requirements specification. This will run to several hundred A4 sheets of typing and will

98 PRACTICAL PROJECT MANAGEMENT

be broken down into volumes. Every page and paragraph is numbered in such a way that it can be uniquely identified. This will be studied by the contractor in the opening weeks of the project. A dialogue will develop between the contractor's technical staff and the customer to iron out ambiguities and to make sure that both sides understand the same thing from the document. At this stage perhaps we should say that the user requirements specification (URS) is expressed in plain language. The URS says what the user expects to give the system and what he expects to receive as output from it. The URS also explains in plain language what decisions or sums the computer is required to perform. Some customers may include in their URS logical tables showing these requirements.

When both sides understand the URS, there is a formal exchange of documents, which defines the project baseline. Because we do not live in a perfect world it may be necessary to exclude some small sections of the URS from the baseline because they cannot be agreed. They are then processed through the change control procedure as amendments to the baseline. The URS becomes the basis of the contract between customer and supplier.


## 10:3  INITIATION OF CHANGE PROPOSAL

Proposals for a change to the URS may be made by the customer, or by the supplier. The proposal is made in writing in simple memorandum form and signed by a manager authorised to request a change. It gives the change a name and has an originator's serial number and date. It may ask for a reply by a specific date. It gives a reference to the part of the URS it is proposed to change and gives details of the change. It may also indicate, when the originator is the customer, that he requires the supplier to proceed to implement the change forthwith if there is no impact on performance, delivery date or cost.

The supplier's project team includes a change controller and all change proposals go to him. He keeps a change proposal register in the form shown in Figure 10.1. The change controller allots a priority, if necessary, after consulting the originator of the proposal and those affected by it. We suggest three levels of priority are used. *Routine* is used for normal proposals that can be handled by the normal process and still produce the reply in sufficient time. At least 80% of all changes should fall into this category. If they don't, something is wrong—either the system is too cumbersome or the orignators are being inefficient and/or unreasonable. *Priority* is used for proposals, where a reply is needed earlier than would be possible if the normal routine process was followed. The change controller will himself have to arrange to short circuit the routine procedures in order to meet the

Name of change _____

Serial number _____ Date _____

Originator _____ Originator date _____

Reference _____

Brief description of proposed change




Routine                    Urgent                    Flash

Date of _____

Circulation to committee _____

First consideration by committee _____ _____

Change control committee decision _____

Date of decision to customer _____

Customer decision _____ Date _____

URS control sheet number _____

URS amendments issued.  Date _____

Other comments




**Figure** IO.I  PROJECT CHANGE CONTROL REGISTER

required decision date. *Flash* must only be used very rarely in circumstances that justify the calling of a special change control committee meeting in addition to their normal cycle of meetings.

## 10:4   CHANGE CONTROL COMMITTEE

The supplier project change control committee is responsible for considering all proposals for change to the URS, evaluating the technical effects of the proposed change and recommending whether the change should be proceeded with or not. It will estimate the effect that the change would have on allocation of resources. Where a project team is working to a critical delivery date the possible need for additional resources and the practicability of incorporating them would be considered. It will estimate the effects of the proposed change on the performance aspects of the project and on the delivery date.

The managers of the main departments or teams contributing to the project or their representatives form the change control committee and the change controller acts as secretary to the committee. The project team network scheduler or progress manager is normally also a member of the committee. Where a representative comes to the committee he must have full authority to speak and act for his manager. The frequency of meetings will be determined by the work load. In the early stages of a project the change committee may well meet as frequently as once a week. The change controller will circulate to each member of the committee details of each change proposal as it is received. He will convene the meetings and issue an agenda to each member and to the project manager before each meeting.

The change controller as secretary, will take minutes of the meetings and circulate them to the committee members, the project manager and such other members of the project team as may be nominated. The minutes should be circulated within twenty-four hours of the meeting being held.

Where the change control committee can decide on a change at the meeting it will record its decision and leave the further processing of the change to the change controller. Where it cannot reach a decision it will appoint a change investigation team of one or more people. The team will be drawn from the departments affected by the change and will obtain all the information necessary for the next meeting of the change control committee to reach a decision.

The change control committee can in effect take one of five actions:

1    Approve the change proposal
2    Ask the originator for more information

3    Refer the proposal to a change investigation team
4    Reject the proposal if the originator is from one of the supplier's own
     departments
5    Recommend rejection of a customer proposal

If a customer proposal is approved and results in no impact on performance, delivery date or cost, this may be put in hand immediately, provided the customer has indicated his consent on his change proposal. In other cases of approval the change controller consults the project manager and whoever is responsible for contract administration. He prices the change. He then sends a formal notification to the customer in writing that the change can be accepted. He says what the impact will be on performance, cost and time-scale. He normally also puts a time limit for acceptance by the customer. This is because as time goes by, the implementation of change normally becomes more expensive and difficult.

When the change controller receives the customer's written acceptance of the impact of change and request to implement the change he in turn checks the original change control committee decision and issues instructions to implement the change. The instructions are supported by a written amendment to the URS. Each amendement should consist of a new complete replacement sheet or sheets of URS, so that the amendment can be accomplished speedily by removing the old sheet and replacing with the new. Each amendment sheet should have a line in the margin indicating which part of the text has changed. The heading information on each sheet should indicate the serial number and date of issue of the sheet. Great care must be taken to see that every sheet of the URS, which is affected by the approved change, is in fact amended.

The change controller must keep a master register showing the latest issue of every sheet in the URS. The change controller must keep a copy of the original URS on which baseline agreement was reached and a copy of every amendment sheet issued. He should keep for each approved change a control sheet which shows which pages of the URS are affected by the change and give the issue number of each amendment page issued. It should also give the reference number of the change proposal and a brief outline of the change and the reason it was required. These control sheets should be retained as a separate volume of the URS. In addition to this the change controller should keep a separate file for each proposed change with all the relevant correspondence. These files must be retained until the customer finally signs-off the project on acceptance and pays all the money due under the contract.

The change control procedure outlined above or something similar is, we believe, essential to the success of any complex project. It requires a considerable amount of time and effort from senior technical management. It also requires considerable administrative effort. It involves significant costs in the field of typing, copying and duplicating. An appreciable amount of storage space is also needed by the change controller. Where major work is subcontracted rather than done by in-house departments, a rather more complicated system for the evaluation of changes will be required so that firm quotations are made for each change across the relevant contract boundary.

In addition to the URS, there will of course also be much documentation specifying how the requirements of the URS will be translated and expanded into program production specifications. Once these have been agreed and issued these will become subject to the same change control procedure as changes to the URS except that where a change is approved by the change control committee it can be implemented forthwith, without reference to the customer in most cases.

Running a tight change control procedure should ensure that the project manager knows what he is trying to do at every stage of the project. It should prevent unauthorised changes. It avoids the situation where changes are initiated without a full recognition of their impact. It also helps to avoid squabbling over contract and price between customer and contractor. Because it focuses attention on changes it also helps to minimise cost increases and project delays. A sound well-operated change control procedure brings undoubted benefits to both contractor and customer. It is obviously costly to operate and the cost must be taken into account in the project budget. In our view the costs are by far outweighed by the benefits.

# Part Four

# PROJECT MANAGEMENT COMMUNICATION

# 11

# Elements of Communication

The project manager will need to operate—within his company and with the customer—effective communication and reporting procedures to help him ensure that the project is proceeding satisfactorily, to adequately appraise management and ensure customer satisfaction. It is not an exageration to say that proper reporting and the setting up of adequate communications is a weakness on many projects. The project manager should therefore look at this problem as a matter of importance. Early setting up is essential so that all the appropriate people are in the communication net straight away. Good habits will then stick.

## 11:1 BASICS

Some of the basics of communication will be considered first. If the subject is understood one has more chance of interpreting the real needs of the situation. Before that, however, one important "need" baseline:

> One of the most important responsibilities of a project manager is to ensure that all parties from their respective direct staff, functional operation or subcontract basis have a clear, unambiguous and common understanding on a continuing basis, of the project, its aims and complete purpose and problems. This facet apart from any other is instrumental in ensuring the highest chance of a successful project by encouraging problem solving and system trade-offs.

It is clear that this responsibility demands good communication but what is "good" communication. Fundamentally, communication is a mutual exchange of facts, thoughts and opinion. It is clear that any business communication must be purposeful and to be effective communication should get the desired response. In project work especially, good communication, properly timed, can turn resistance into co-operation.

It is equally clear that from the very definition of a manager (having to get things done through other people), communication is a major task of any manager. It directly affects work relationships, upwards, downwards and sideways. Upwards to notify or report or to receive help, sideways for co-ordination and ensuring, downwards to give plans and schedules.

There are certain rules for good or effective communication which, if regularly followed, do help greatly to ensure success.

1    The real message must be *short*: it must not be hidden in a wealth of non important and time consuming verbiage. Anything that does not add to the value of the message should be excluded

2    Information should be *meaningful*, understandable, strike the right chord in such matters as importance and relevance to the situation

3    Naturally the communication must be *factual*. It must also appear factual. Some facts are written in such a way as to be suspect

4    No *ambiguity* must exist in the message

5    Communication must be *convincing*

In all communication the project manager must express, convey and exude confidence, knowledge and respect for his profession. It is not "telling" people that ensures communication success. It is the ensuring that understanding exists so that the desired response can be obtained. As we cannot effectively change other people we have to change, if necessary, our own methods of communication to ensure understanding in others. Because communication is so vital it is equally vital that we should make strenuous efforts to understand how we can ensure that we can communicate.

If a bricklayer told you that company *A* was a good company to invest in you would probably wonder how this man should know. If a well-known city editor or stockbroker mentioned it you might still not invest but you would probably not doubt the source.

The credibility of the communicator is important bearing in mind the content of the message. The motive is important and both items influence the receiver's reactions.

If the bricklayer, on the other hand, told you that brick type $Z$ was better than type $Y$ you would accept the motive as helpful and the credibility would be in little doubt.

If a project manager wants to strike the right chord either to get the maximum effectiveness out of his staff, the functional staffs or higher management, he must remember a few simple means obtained by studying people who have done a lot of influencing of people in their time.

Reinforce your audience belief. If the receiver is already inclined to believe some of the facts, prove those first and then build on them. Obviously success is always a good builder. State firm conclusions from the facts built up and firmly call for action.

People are likely to be more effective and more interested if common interests can be stressed. An effective project manager should, without actually becoming a crusader, get people to really believe in the project, catch their interest by things, ideas; people are influenced by group belonging or wanting to belong.

Make people want to belong—they are then more susceptible to want communication and respond to it.

If you study advertising practices you will observe that most advertisers keep pegging away at the same old theme day after day. It is possible to learn from the advertisers.

Communicate where it is possible, little by little over a time. Repetition prolongs the influence of the message.

It is clear that one must be careful in business communications not to overdo this otherwise one of the other factors may be damaged—for example, credibility of the sender. In writing to people, try to keep to short sentences, use familiar words and not too much jargon. Use active verbs and above all make your message interesting and persuasive. If you want to make the most impact, oral presentation is more effective for changing opinions.

11:2  LISTENING

It seems more easy to talk than listen. The other fellow, it is clear, cannot explain it as well as you can; you understand what he means when he is halfway through so why wait until he has finished, in any case you have heard it all before so there is no need to really listen any more; what he says does not really make sense anyway and has little bearing on the present situation, and you have not got time to listen any longer. Feel guilty? This happens to everybody without exception and managers must be continually on their guard against such feelings. There is no doubt that it is difficult sometimes with a slow speaker who is actually off the target but you have a large part to play in listening to that man. Listening does not mean just saying nothing but it does mean very limited talking while the other man says his piece. One can, however, ask such questions as:"Would you just explain that again perhaps from a different viewpoint?" or "Would you expand on that particular item?" or "I believe I understand you as follows, please tell me if I am right . . . ."

These are questions to get clarification and are thus still under the heading of listening. Try always to be 100% sure you understand what has been said. Think of the problems in a simple two-man conversation and you get some idea of the problems of communications. The speaker says what he believes are the words which convey what he thinks. They may not be absolutely clear. The listener interprets the words as his mind tells him to do. The speaker puts feeling into his words, how he feels about what he says. This feeling may not strike a chord in the listener. The speaker's voice is toned to convey an attitude to the words being used. The tone may be meaningless, meaningful, insulting or soothing to the listener. The speaker, in his general manner of talking, conveys an intention towards the listener. The latter may regard this as friendly, neutral or hostile.

The reactions of the listener must be kept in mind all the time if one is concerned to make a maximum impact with communication.

Another big problem for the listener is "generalised listening." This is not so much a direct mental barrier but more like a rough form of scrambler. It can arise if you suddenly think you've heard all this before. When one does that the scrambling starts and the speaker's voice becomes a noise. Occasionally one may come back to concentration but in the meantime one may miss some very important point. Don't let the surface mind shut off the message; keep concentration high. When the mind has absorbed the message then digest it and see what a proper mental look at it reveals. There may not be a lot you have heard before; there may be just one item worth its weight in gold.

One problem we all face is the length of time taken to say a simple thing to somebody else. Most people take in only about 20% of what they hear and about 30% of what they see and the average attention span before a break is only some fifteen seconds in a conversation, so these are natural obstacles that have to be got around. One must watch carefully for the best time to make the maximum impact with important messages especially in reporting upwards. If when the message is given it can also be illustrated then the 20% heard + 30% seen = 50% impact, which is much better.

## 11:3 OBSTACLES TO COMMUNICATION

Its easy to think negatively or so it would seem from the sort of thought processes one sees at times. Negative thinking is something that tends to kill off good communication. It is a type of reaction—for example, a works manager is explaining to his works superintendent how he believes a certain machine can be used to better advantage. The immediate reaction is: "but it has never been done that way before." It is an honest reply not meant to be awkward or an obstacle but typical of the way so many people react. The positive way of thinking about the same situation would be to question the works manager to make sure of what he is really saying. After that one should see how it would be possible to try out the proposition to see if it really is better. The theme of positive thought is: "how can we achieve something," not "we have not done it that way before." Another range of obstacles is the "he won't like it" attitude. Now "he" can be a whole range of people from the customer to the managing director. The truth of the matter in 99 cases out of a 100 is that no one has ever asked the person concerned whether he likes it or not.

Other obstacles to communication stem from the following:

1  Fear that what has to be communicated is going to rebound in some way that is unpleasant. This type of reaction is often found in companies where empire building and immature management is at work
2  Where resistance to change is high, no one wants to communicate in case they make the change seem justifiable. Lack of a communication policy in the company or broken promises by management in the past
3  Unclear messages, complex language or jargon, muddled or too lengthy messages or inopportune timing. From a positive point of view a few well-chosen policies on communication and then ensuring that they are put into effect will work wonders. For example:

*a*  Management support and determination
*b*  Sound planning, coupled to the needs of the business, of a communication policy
*c*  The setting up of suitable channels and media to ensure good communication

*d*    The knowledge that overcommunication, unless it is carried to excess, is far less harmful than undercommunication

With undercommunication the danger of a communication vacuum exists; into such a vacuum will come flooding rumours and bad communication.

## 11:4  STAFF COMMUNICATION

In dealing with staff one is likely to be involved in one or more of five different modes of communication:

1    Telling staff to do something
2    Telling them about something
3    Guiding them in some way
4    Discussing common problems
5    Listening to their personal or work problems

If one is communicating properly in all the above one will ask questions to get all the right facts or make sure one really does understand the things that are being said. The worst sort of remark to make is something like: "You know the trouble with you Bill is . . . ." Immediately the receiver of such a statement is on his guard and it may take some considerable time before easy communication becomes possible again.

In telling staff to do something it should be done in such a way that they can understand the reasons for the statements if this is possible to do. Most people want to understand but if one does not make the attempt to communicate then it may look as though one does not want to and this starts the vicious circle. One is always more sure of getting a sensible response if one leads people to a conclusion rather than simply telling them something, especially if they do not like the thing that is being said. This does not mean that any hiding of the truth had to be done but they, to act properly on instructions, have to understand, to agree the conclusion to be a right one. They have to say to themselves: "The message is clear, the reasons are sensible, I do not particularly like the message but my job is to do what I am told."

## 11:5  MANAGEMENT COMMUNICATION

A manager wants information in the fastest time practicable provided it is factual and meaningful. Timeliness is obviously important. Old information on current problems is a sure way to fall out with your boss unless he asks for it. The other facets of good basic communication were mentioned earlier and they are very appropriate in this sort of communication. No boss, for instance, wants to plough his way through a mass of reading to find your well hidden facts, golden though they be.

The manager wants to hear any information on divergence of plans. These include budgets, time plans, or performance of agreed work objectives. He will want to know whether any divergencies are temporary and for how long and whether the original plan is going to suffer in the long term. He will also want to hear of significant acheivements in the performance of your work as these add credence to both your and his efforts towards the total objectives. One point is important. Managers do have different preferred methods of how they like to be told things. It is worth finding out what your manager prefers. Communication then gets that much easier.

The project manager must see to the communication problem immediately he takes over the project and use all the good principles of communication in terms of media, reports, methods, instructions, project definitions, and relationships with all people. The PM is in the centre of a hub of communication (see Figure 11.1).

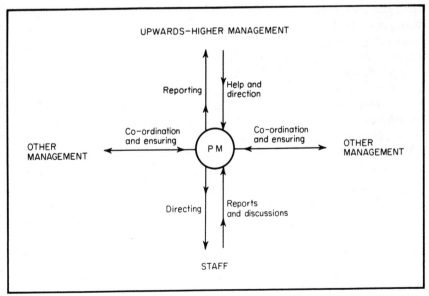

Figure 11.1 COMMUNICATION FLOWS

# 12

# Project Management Meetings and Reporting

## 12:1 CLARITY OF REPORTING

Pride and ability are two of the very qualities which, among others, project managers ought to possess, but which, strangely, can menace the success of their projects. What has to be recognised right at the start by all project managers is that some limits exist as to their power to apply resources and make certain decisions. It must also be recognised that to admit this is not a weakness but a strength—a sign of good management.

This knowledge should influence the way a project manager reports to higher management. If help is needed it is his duty to ask for it, fast. The project is the thing, he must nurture and protect it. Management has a right to know that help is needed before it is too late and customer satisfaction lost, or likely to be lost.

Do not spring surprises on higher management. Too bureaucratic an approach is not a good idea but an ordered regime is necessary in meetings and reporting. To that extent regularity and some standardisation of reporting procedures is essential.

Figure 12.1 is a recognised management summary report which itself can have backing information. The first page is a summary report and must not be too long otherwise the important issues (as shown seen in the chapter on communication) can be clouded. Whether the format used for Figure 12.1 is suitable for your work is immaterial; it can be changed, but do include the sections that can clearly report to management:

| PROJECT MANAGEMENT SUMMARY REPORT | Page 1 of | Number |
|---|---|---|

Date_____     Project number_____

Description_____     Project manager_____

**1 Progress during report period**

State what was accomplished and scheduled during the month. A comparison should be made of the schedule milestones with the actual milestone accomplishments and the current predictions as shown in the schedule section of the management summary report.

**2 Problems**

Briefly note any management, technical or administrative problems that are causing, or might cause, technical changes, schedule slippage and/or cost difficulties. Do not give a detailed discussion of minor technical problems. This report is a channel for alerting higher management to problems with appropriate assistance and/or action from, or by, them. The problem discussion may include other areas such as facilities, manpower, funding, changes in scope, interfaces or other contractual matters. Relate cost and/or schedule variance with the problems that are creating them.

**3 Plans for next period**

Briefly state what is planned and what can be realistically anticipated during the next report period. Plans should include remedial courses of action developed to correct existing problems, covering what action, by whom, when, and the expected effect.

Signed_____

**Figure I2.I PROJECT STATUS REPORT**

1    Significant progress
2    Problems
3    Plans

Behind this summary sheet should be included a simple macronet of key
activities or a bar chart derived from the latest macronet if that is more
acceptable. What is required is one simple picture of the up-to-date position
and it does not matter how it is done.

Accompanying this should be a financial control document showing
clearly actual and/or committed costs against budget and coupled with
accomplishment as described in the previous chapter. Backing these can
be special reports which may expand any particular management, technical or commercial point. Also included should be a staff situation report.

Keep page one simple, clear and factual. Management must see bad news
as well as good news.


## 12:2   CUSTOMER MEETINGS AND REPORTING

There has to be set up with the customer an agreed meetings and reporting
system. These must be rigidly adhered to; they must also be frank and
honest. Very rarely does lack of honesty with the customer pay off. If there
are problems, talk them over with the customer. We have found that even in
very tightly bound commercial situations this approach does pay off because
a mutual trust is rapidly established.

The majority of customers are not in business to extract penalties un-
fairly or even at all if they can avoid it. Obviously if the supplier stays
clearly in the wrong, is permanently late, or cannot perform as agreed in the
end event, then that is what the contract is for. However, it is often possible
for trade-offs to occur; the customer may not be perfect in the use of the
product or service; his requirements may have changed.

A project manager on top of his job will use the frank exchanges at the
meetings to point out variations and trade them against any shortfall he
may have until an agreed balance is obtained. This is business and it avoids
unpleasant and expensive litigation that could arise if things are left to
slide into late and serious argument. This argument does bring out one
vital necessity: the man on the customer side must be capable of dealing
properly, he must have the authority of the customer.

Too often project managers deal at too low a level in the customer
management tree. Get the customer meetings and reporting organised from
the start at the right level. It may be appropriate to hold them once a
month but if the project manager thinks once a week is necessary then he

should arrange it. If it needs a daily meeting then have it. One excuse one must never accept from any project manager is that he has not managed to see the customer lately when a problem has been left to fester.

As well as meetings the customer is entitled to receive formal reports, both of the meetings and about progress. This is a matter for the project manager to handle carefully; any trade-offs between him and the customer must be correctly noted and incorporated in the report so that an accurate and fair picture is built up.

It is important that the customer, both at the meetings and through the reports, must be in no doubt about the matter, extent and timing of his responsibilities in the project.

## 12:3   PROJECT MEETINGS

It seems hardly necessary to say that the project team must communicate effectively among themselves to ensure that no "holes" are left. Some deliberate overlapping should take place to take care of holidays, sickness, etc. The project cannot be allowed to suffer because of what in the main is a predictable problem.

As part of the communication process the project manager should hold regular, say weekly, progress meetings. These meetings should cover in a fairly formal manner all the management, technical and other items appertaining to the project. Management is the key to many items because unless good technical processes are properly managed the efforts can be wasted. The project manager must always remember that he is a manager not a technician, however competent he may be in one particular technical aspect.

Because any project with a project manager is likely to be of a size where the commercial implications are important it is essential that a project filing system is set up. Situation reports must be retained for reference with work sheets used to compile the information recorded on the formal reports. There will be a judgement made as to the extent of this filing and clerical activity but it should be remembered that it is no economy to save £5000 on this and then not be able to support a claim for £10 000 worth of extra work or the complete rejection of a penalty claim.

In reporting in and around the project, a straightforward checklist is probably as good as any other. If the network is large and computer run, then almost any type of progressing printout desired can be forthcoming. If handworking is used it can be formatted like a computer printout (see virtually any book on PERT for this—there is nearly always an example). Alternatively a simple list of key items and dates may be sufficient, provided the items are really key items and have the proper significance to the project and to management. What is important is that meaningful, up-to-date and factual simplicity is to be preferred to sophisticated methods half done. What has to be shown essentially, are three dates or times, every time the project is progressed:

1    The planned date (or time)
2    The achieved date (or time)
3    The trend situation stemming from these two.

In other words what was planned, what was achieved and what is likely to be achieved using historic information as one input.

In large projects using much artisan labour, simple bar charts, key date lists and other means are best because they restrict the information to that necessary. Computer printouts may be all-embracing but to someone who either is not used to reading them or who does not particularly want to get used to reading them, they usually look like yards of paper with a lot of surplus information. In a project using a smaller number of people, where the technical skills are higher, and for the project manager and his direct staff, the computer printout is highly convenient with its many printout variations.

## 12:4   COMPANY MEETINGS

Again at regular intervals—say monthly or two-monthly, as the situation appears to demand—meetings must be held with the functional organisations in the company engaged in supplying or supporting the project. A lot of work manifestly must be done continually outside of meetings but every so often the appropriate company managers or their accredited representatives must be brought together to review carefully the next phase of the plans to anticipate any difficulties. Problem solving on the past plans will have been done as they occurred; these meetings are primarily for forward reviewing and to see what lessons can be drawn from past experience on this and other projects.

It is interesting to note how few people want to really take note of previous experience in their own and other companies. While we are great advocates of value analysis—questioning always old values—this sometimes takes much effort and time to break through into new solutions. In the meantime we have only got this past experience to go on. An example of what we mean is the installation of some heavy and complex machinery. Perhaps it takes ten weeks to install. The company now brings out a new machine of equal complexity although some of its functions are improved.

How long is it going to take to install? We have an engineering friend who had this sort of problem and he received several different estimates ranging from five to ten weeks. Why less than ten weeks? What is the evidence to support it? If other companies take five weeks then it is time something was done about it but if they take ten as well it is likely that that is the practical time. This does not mean one should not strive to beat the time if it is important to do so but one should always be able to justify differences otherwise one can lose time and money by trying to achieve unachievable targets.

# 13

# Supplier and Customer Relationship

In considering the subject of project management, there is one aspect that should be not overlooked. Every project is executed with a view to its being of value to some user or customer. A bridge will be taken over and maintained by some public authority, a new university will be taken over and operated by the university authority, a dedicated computer project will be handed over to the service operator, a motel will be handed over to a hotel manager. In every case, although the project has a limited life cycle, the product of that project normally has a user who has a continuing use for it.

The most clear-cut case is where one company acts as main contractor for the project, which in due course is handed over to another company or organisation. There is a fairly straightforward customer–supplier relationship. This chapter will examine this relationship and the part that the customer should play in his project. Although the customer–supplier relationship is more clear-cut, the same principles apply when a project is executed in-house on behalf of another department of the same organisation. With internal projects there is, in practice, a tendency for fuzzy relationships to develop, thus creating an ideal climate for project delays and increases of cost. Ideally responsibilities should be clear-cut. In the case of an internal project, there is a strong case for a notional contract between the user or commissioning department and the project manager.

## 13:1 SUCCESSFUL PROJECTS

Elsewhere in this book we have given as our definition of a successful project, one that is completed to specification, within budget and on time. There is, however, another possible definition. A successful project is one that satisfies the customer. You may think that this is only the other side of the same coin. But in fact it is common to find a customer who is perfectly satisfied, notwithstanding considerable deviation from the originally forecast performance, cost and delivery. Similarly it is possible to find customers who have been given what they asked for at the expected cost and delivered on time, who are nonetheless highly dissatisfied.

The customer has a great deal to contribute to the success of his own project. In many cases he does not appreciate the part he should play. This is common, for instance, with computer projects. In these cases it is part of the project manager's duty to educate the customer.

## 13:2  DEFINITION OF USER REQUIREMENTS

The first major contribution which the customer should make is a clear definition of his requirements. If this has been produced before the contract for the project is placed, this is ideal. However, it is very common for a project to be started and an order placed for its implementation before the requirements have been specified in detail. In this case the project manager must press for the provision of the requirements specification as early as practicable, making clear that his delivery date and price are dependent upon its receipt. In the extreme case, the project manager must himself define the user requirements and obtain the customer's agreement—in writing—that the definition does in fact define his requirements.

## 13:3  PROJECT ACCEPTANCE

The other major and related contribution from the customer is final acceptance of the project. This may seem a very early stage at which to start talking of acceptance. However, unless the customer intends just to take the word of his contractor that he has finished, acceptance can be a major undertaking. It has to be planned from a very early stage in the project.

In the case of the LACES project, the customer placed a main contract with ICL for about £3½ million worth of computer equipment, programs and terminals. The customer, the Post Office, devoted about thirty-four man-years to preparing and carrying out the system acceptance tests. Quite apart from this, considerable effort was put into the normal standard engineering acceptance tests of the computer hardware and terminals.

From this you may see that customer acceptance tests are a serious—and expensive—contribution to an advanced technology project. They have their place in any project. In some, acceptance has to be done in stages.

For instance, in a building project, the foundations will be accepted before they are buried by the progress of the building.

Apart from the requirements definition and contract—which establish the baseline from which the contractor works and the acceptance tests which mark the technical culmination of the project—the customer has a continuing interest in the project. He may be required to make progress payments. He may wish to change the user-requirements specification. Most important of all, he will have his own plans for putting the results of the project to work. These plans may well have to be dovetailed into the progress of the project.

For most projects, the customer will have a manager who is responsible for the project even if it is not his sole task. He may be a line manager who will in due course become the principal user. He may be appointed full time, specifically to control the project. If there is more than one main contractor or if there is a substantial amount of work to be done in-house by the customer, then he will probably appoint his own project manager. In some cases he may appoint an outside consultant or professional firm to represent his interest. Whatever the situation may be for any particular project, the supplier's project manager must establish who the customer's authorised representative is. The project manger and his team will undoubtedly have dealings with many people amongst the customer's staff, but there must be one man who, for all normal matters, speaks (and writes) for the customer.

It is also essential to establish who on the customer's side can give agreement to changes to the user-requirements specification. The customer has to appreciate that such changes may well have an impact on the project performance, delivery date and cost. The person on the customer side who can authorise change to the specification, must be senior enough to consider the acceptability of these impacts on the customer. The situation where he authorises a change only to be overruled by someone more senior in his own organisation cannot and must not be tolerated. A change once ordered by the customer, is implemented unless it is cancelled by another approved change—which may well have a further cost and timescale impact because of the waste of resources involved.

The relationship between customer and contractor should normally involve a formal mechanism of meetings and reports as well as the formal change control procedure. Depending upon the nature and stage of the project, there should be regular meetings between the customer's project manager and the supplier's project manager to discuss progress, problems and future plans. It is also frequently a good idea to have a steering committee. This should meet once a month and be chaired by a very senior member of the customer's staff, possibly, if the project is large relative to the size of the customer's operations, it may be chaired by the managing director. Whoever it is, it must be someone of considerable seniority and "fire power" within the customer's organisation.

Represented on the steering committee should be the managers of all the customer's divisions that will be affected by the project. The customer's project manager (or nominated manager) should act as secretary to the steering group. If the customer has enlisted the help of a consultant or of a professional firm of some sort, then they should also be present. The contractor will be represented by the project manager and such of his team as he may consider necessary, having regard to the agenda for the particular meeting. The contractor may also be represented by a member of his senior management. The main aim of the steering committee is to keep the customer's progress in line with the main project work and to bring problems or difficulties into the open. Practice, of course, varies and in some projects the steering committee may exercise a degree of executive authority, particularly where there is considerable customer involvement. Where more than one main contractor is involved, they may both be represented on the steering committee.

In some projects, where the customer is, in effect, a consortium of users, then the steering committee may well be the executive authority dealing direct with a single main contractor for both project and subsequent operating phase. This is a type of project that we expect to be seen more frequently in the future. For instance, we expect to see more large multinational projects where several governments or their nominated agents are the customer. Similarly, in the computer field, we expect to see more projects where a project develops to satisfy particular functions for a number of independant users.

LACES is an early but perhaps typical project of this kind. Here some 187 independent firms—international airlines and freight agents—got together with HM Customs and Excise to sponsor a project to simplify and speed up the procedures connected with importing cargo through the Heathrow Airport, London. Every firm had an interest in the project and its future methods of working. The steering group was the sole project authority. It consisted of representative of all three groups of users—airlines, agents and HM Customs as well as the National Data Processing Service of the Post Office, that was main contractor for the project. The steering group was the formal authority for the issue of the requirements specification and for formally approving all changes. It met monthly. In consequence there was a special procedure for obtaining formal consent for urgent charges. The main contractor then had his own liaison and control procedures for the control of his principal subcontractors for the building and computer work as well as his own staff working on the project.

How far should the project manager keep the customer informed about problems and slippages? We believe that in the long run a policy of absolute honesty pays. In a complex project, once you start concealing problems and delays, you get into considerable difficulties. The customer is bound to find out unless the trouble is rectified in a very short space of time. As Sam O'Donavan has said, it is in the nature of life that things go wrong whenever the opportunity arises and in the most embarrassing way possible. Hence the very problem, which you choose to conceal from your customer is likely to prove intractable. Once he finds out that you have attempted to conceal it from him your credibility will be destroyed. It is far better to tell him the truth from the beginning. He may complain bitterly about poor progress and delays but as he sees that you are not concealing things from him and that you have the situation under control, his confidence in you is likely to grow rather than diminish. If this sort of trusting relationship can be built up in the early stages of the project it will stand you in good stead in later stages when you meet serious trouble.

We advocate a policy of complete project visibility—that is, the customer has access to the progress reports coming in to the project manager and can inspect all project documents, even those in draft form. This means that he can see problems as soon as you can. In practice if the project manager is capable he will see the problem before the customer, notwithstanding full visibility. His ability to spot trouble in its early stages and his ability to get remedial action in hand promptly should help to cement the customer's faith in him.

This business of building up the customer's confidence in the project manager is of considerable importance. Mistakes can be made and things can go wrong at any stage of a project. In some ways, of course, the most fundamental mistakes can be made in the earliest stages of a project. But even in the best-run projects, serious problems can arise in the final months. It is at this stage that a considerable amount of capital is tied up unproductively in the project by both customer and contractor. At this stage the correction of errors can be costly and time consuming. If there is a degree of trust and confidence between project manager and customer it is easier to deal with some of the tricky situations that arise at this stage than if there is an atmosphere of suspicion and distrust.

This spirit of confidence and mutual co-operation is one of the basic requirements for success in any large or complex project, particularly so when many different parties are involved. Some people try to create this spirit by lavish entertaining. This is an unnecessary expense in most cases, and, apart from anything else, lavish entertaining is time consuming as well as costly. Even a heavy lunch is sufficient to reduce the afternoon's thought processes. By the time that the project manager gets down to work his company probably has a signed contract and the customer wants to see results. Some modest entertainment will certainly help. When work is occupying extended hours or is carrying on overnight or at weekends, customers staff, as well as your own, will appreciate a drink or a snack.

Great care must be taken where the customer is a government department or nationalised industry. State servants, particularly in Britain, are very sensitive to the suggestion that they may be susceptible to bribery or other corrupt practices. They may feel that they have to return the project manager's hospitality and may be very restricted in their ability to do so. Even the top ranks of the civil service are not encouraged to be extravagant and lower down the heirarchy they are severely restricted. To avoid any feeling of awkwardness it may be advisable to entertain at about the same level as is permitted to them. Lavishness should be avoided even when the customer is another company.

Where a working meeting of ten or twelve people takes place regularly, it can soon result in a substantial bill if all present at the meeting are taken out to lunch and drinks each time. If practicable there is much to be said for making it a true working lunch and having sandwiches and a bottle of beer—or wine or lemonade—brought into the office. What is valuable, however, is for the project manager to lunch regularly with the customer's responsible manager, perhaps once a month. It can be quite a modest lunch but it can be an opportunity for informal discussion. Both parties can bring out the points that worry them without any formal confrontation. Perhaps the customer feels that Mr *A* on the project team is being discourteous and upsetting some of the customer staff. Perhaps the project manager feels that someone on the customer side is being inefficient or deliberately obstructive. Dealt with formally at a regular meeting, or by correspondence, defensive walls are likely to be erected immediately. However, in the informal atmosphere of a private lunch, they can be brought into the open with benefit to both sides.

The project manager must try to build up the community of interest between himself and his opposite number on the customer side. Together they must try to develop a project view point. It is always difficult for two or more organisations to work towards a common aim, particularly when their interests may to some extent be divergent. The contractor wants his profit and the customer wants his project at the least practicable cost. Nonetheless there really is a common aim—the success of the project—and if the

124 PRACTICAL PROJECT MANAGEMENT

two people chiefly concerned on the customer and contractor sides can develop a community of interest, this goes a long way to swinging their organisations into line in support of the project.

Keeping really close to the customer and understanding him is part of the project manager's job. He must develop a feel for the customer's real needs and interests. He must know when something is so vital to the customer that he will stick on it. Equally it is helpful to appreciate which things are of lesser importance to the customer and where he may be prepared to concede a little. It helps also to develop a feel for the customers timescales and financial commitments. Where has he a month's float? Where are his serious financial commitments? If a one-month delay in delivering a certain phase of the project can result in the customer being unable to use it for six months, this must be appreciated. It is a help in getting close to the customer if you can persuade him to provide you with an office on his premises—preferably close to the manager responsible for the project within the customer organisation. If the customer has a canteen or managers' dining-room, try to make use of it as much as you are able. The idea must be to become an accepted part of the background so that people talk naturally in front of you.

## 13:4 CONTROL OF CHARGES

If the work can conveniently be done from the customer's offices, there is a lot to be said for getting as many of your team as practicable into his premises. If, as is frequently the case, he does not charge for his accommodation and services, it helps to keep down your costs. Even if he does charge you, it is still worth getting as many of your team as possible into his premises. It helps to develop the close working spirit of co-operation, which is necessary. Also junior tongues sometimes wag more freely than more senior ones. Make sure your team feed back to you any information they glean.

A successful conclusion to your project requires both formality and informality. The informality helps to promote the project spirit of co-operation and common endeavour. However, it must not lead to slackness in certain essentials. In most projects, there are certain things that have to be done by the customer by certain dates. The initial tender and subsequent contract should have made these perfectly clear and should also have made clear that the contractor's undertaking relative to cost and delivery are dependent upon the customer meeting these commitments. The project manager must then hold the customer to these dates. If they are missed then the fact must be promptly recorded in a formal note to the customer.

There are, of course, some cases where the project delay will not be in proportion to the delay in completing an intermediate dependency. One week's delay in providing some facility may, because of other factors, lead to a delay of several weeks in project completion. Delay inevitably also means extra cost to the customer and this must be tactfully but firmly pointed out. In practice you may be able to swallow up a short delay by careful contingency planning or the use of your own float. Even in this case, make sure that the customer's delinquency is formally recorded. He may not be so lenient with your shortcomings later in the project, so it pays to have his shortcomings on record.

One serious problem that can arise in the situation when the contractor's project manager decides that the customer project manager is not up to his job. This can be an extremely tricky situation, calling for considerable care as well as tact. In our experience, the customer's manager has to be really bad before it is worth doing anything about it. In one case we were concerned with, there was a manager, Mr *B*, who had done a lot of the preliminary work on the project. The customer's managing director and Mr *C*, one of his senior colleagues, asked our opinion of Mr *B*. We spoke highly of him but said that he lacked certain characteristics that would be important in the project manager. A few days later Mr *B* and Mr *C* had a violent row in the course of which our comments were repeated. Mr *B* in due course did become the customer's project manager and never forgave us. Fortunately that was one project we were able to hand over to someone else to complete.

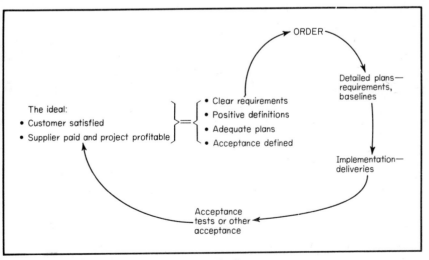

Figure 13.1 PROJECT AND SUCCESS CYCLE

We know of several similar cases. Any attempt to dislodge the customer's manager reaches his ears sooner or later and he will naturally feel aggrieved and antagonistic. This leads to an uncooperative atmosphere in which either you or he must go if the project is to prosper.

To sum up, the customer has a very real and valid interest in the project. After all, he who pays the piper calls the tune. He also has a contribution to make to the project's success and, if necessary, must be persuaded or educated into it. A good relationship between customer's and contractor's project manager is essential to project success. This relationship can only be built on mutual trust and respect. In the project cycle shown in Figure 13.1 supplier and customer must complete the success cycle as well.

# Part Five

# COMMERCIAL ISSUES

# 14

# The Tender

While it does not befall every project manager to be involved in the actual tender, a knowledge of the process shows the project manager what he has to complete in implementing the task. All business actions are but links in the chain of ideas turned into profit; it is wise for all links to know something about the others. The tender includes items where the project manager has to protect his company's interests and he should know about them. The object of tendering for the supply of any goods or services must be the hope of ultimate reward over and above the costs involved. It should be, therefore, a continuous search for the finely balanced price which gives optimum profit in terms of successful tenders and the actual cash returns. Success invariably comes to those who have the essential ingredients:

1  Knowledge of their company costs and overheads
2  Experience to properly assess the risks
3  Knowledge of the market-place
4  Ability to negotiate the right contract
5  The company administration, facilities and resources to carry out the contract properly

Before returning to examine these ingredients in more detail, we should briefly look at the main sources from which tenders may emanate.

*Production industry.*  Many industries are geared to what is essentially a set range of goods from a production line. The production is in accordance with a market plan worked out well in advance. There are large numbers of such industries ranging from furniture to computers. Production quantities and types of output can be changed but such change is not easy or quick because of the relative rigidity of large-scale production. Prices are fixed to provide the necessary profit based on the market plan, the knowledge of the market place, and costs of production and overheads. Any one factor can, of course, upset the amount of profit. If the market plan was optimistic, finished stocks might be accumulated until the production line quantities could be reduced. In any event the cash flow will suffer and profits fall. The budgeted costs may get out of hand and again profits fall.

*Engineering and shipbuilding.*   Another group of industries, both large and small, are best exemplified by general engineering and shipbuilding. The bulk of the work is by single projects or tasks as in the shipbuilding case or by set runs of work very often undertaken as a subcontract to a larger contractor in general engineering. In both these cases men, facilities and resources rely on a constant flow of orders dependent on the timescale of each job. Much of the work will be by fixed price quotations. Overstocking of finished goods is not the problem this time but non-utilisation of plant and men soon applies heavy costs to the concern and a remedy will have to be found. This sort of problem has been starkly demonstrated over the last decade in the shipbuilding industry.

*Building and civil engineering.*   The building and civil engineering fields have different problems. They may not have large numbers of permanent staff but obtaining the right labour at the right time and avoiding penalties for jobs overruns are difficult tasks.

There are other sources of tendering but in project management the three already mentioned above cover a large bulk of the total.

## 14:1   KNOWLEDGE OF COSTS AND OVERHEADS

It should be clear to all of us that in the long term successful tendering cannot begin without a detailed knowledge of costs. Only in this way can a true estimated profit be determined, sufficient to sustain dividends and help finance expansion. Many companies would claim that they do know their costs but often such knowledge is of too elementary a nature. The knowledge must be good enough to answer the question: "how low can we mark the price and yet acceptance of the project at that price still be a good thing for the company?" To be answered properly this question demands a high degree of common sense in the company accounting because figures can prove almost anything.

The cost of manufacturing an item in a company appears to be a straightforward calculation but the number of variances that can apply are legion. To keep costs at a minimum requires a continuous examination of short-, medium- and long-term loadings of production. Take too much at uneconomic prices and direct losses result. Take too little work and up go the overheads and consequent drops in profit or actual losses occur.

While not all project staff have to be involved in this knowledge of costs they should be familiar with and interested in the subject; good accountancy might be the basis of the cost knowledge in the tender but this can all be wasted by poor project implementation and lack of understanding. An example of the sort of knowledge that might make the difference between success and failure is the question of guarantees. Suppose the customer wants a longer guarantee and the company wants the order. How much is a longer guarantee worth? This is where knowledge of the cost of providing guarantees would be essential because to provide a longer one is tantamount to a discount but how much? The knowledge of the maintenance failure rate is necessary.

*New or development items.* The incorporation of these into a project requires care; it has been the undoing of many a company because of optimistic estimates of time and money to be expended. To embark on a fixed price contract in these days of inflation without having new development to contend with is bad enough but to embark on a heavy load of development into new areas of technology under the same conditions can indeed be folly. If the work is firmly based on development already concluded the risks are less. A contingency must always be allowed. In all cases of substantial development a development contract should be aimed for; if this approach fails some sort of cost dependency in the price structure is sensible. The project manager must look carefully at such projects as far as implementation is concerned and decide what firm advice must be offered to his senior management. The risk of new management and organisational changes should also not be underestimated.

## 14:2 EXPERIENCE TO PROPERLY ASSESS THE RISKS

Every industry has its own special problems as well as those that are common to all industries. We have just mentioned the guarantee extension question, this is, for example, a common demand in Eastern Europe. It seems perfectly logical to the questioner to ask for increased guarantees across the negotiating table but only experience of what that means, and the costs, can ensure safe answers.

The obvious question that comes to mind under this heading of experience is whether a task similar to that being tendered for has been done before either by your company or another. Are there new areas of development or research? Are there any new problems in engineering, manufacture, shipping, maintenance or commercial agreements? In our previous book, *Successful Project Management*, we detailed the "key techniques" that include this question of defining in detail just what the task is all about. Because of the obvious differences in industry we can only mention these broad areas in order to provoke further thought. From our own work we have found that a great deal worth quantifying can be quantified if there is a will to do it, so that risk assessment becomes far less like crystal-ball gazing. Nevertheless there must in the end be some risks where only "guessing" can help and this is likely to be the case as long as technology continues to advance.

What is often overlooked in risk assessment is the management factor. A vacillating management or an incompetent project manager can be a great risk. This factor must be honestly faced and something done about it if any concern is felt. A general failing in many companies has been not to recognise the size and scope of a particular project and organise the management and planning of it accordingly.

Subcontractors always create some risk and as far as possible the main contract stemming from the tender must be reflected into the subcontracts. It is not always possible to achieve this completely. (If it is it is called a transparent contract.)

## 14:3  KNOWLEDGE OF THE MARKET-PLACE

This ranges through the basic knowledge of what proportion of the market can be usefully considered as open to real competition: what areas are the right ones to cover? What proportion of money should be spent on cultivating these areas? When it is worth stretching out for a new market or to keep an old one? As far as the tender itself is concerned: what competition is there? what chance is there? should the price be tight or not?

## 14:4  ABILITY TO NEGOTIATE THE RIGHT CONTRACT

We don't mean the eyeball-to-eyeball contact across the negotiating table. We are more concerned with the behind-the-scenes attitude of the company commercial department and project manager. They must use their risk experience, knowledge of the market-place and their company's facilities to ensure that a suitable contract is constructed. In many companies a standard contract is aimed at and if a set range of goods is being supplied a standard contract is often possible. In the one-off projects it can be more difficult.

Most people's attitude to the difficult situations is to get as many of their standard clauses into the contract as possible and minimise the non-standard bits. This is obviously a good start, but this part is fairly easy. It is the very non-standard clauses that can cause all the trouble.

The central theme of the negotiation is responsibility and aftercare. All companies may well believe they would like to promise to do something without having any penalty for lateness or not meeting the specification and not having any problem of aftercare once the job is finished and the money obtained. Such an attitude, if allowed, could also be disastrous. The customer, on the other hand, thinks he is being eminently reasonable in demanding a penalty for lateness or non-compliance with the specification and a complete guarantee of trouble-free operation for a specific period. Between these two extremes lies the battlefield of the actual negotiations, but the negotiators on both sides have to know what their final lines of defence are. For the supplier, the ability to negotiate the right contract lies in his experience of previous contracts, as stated earlier, and his assessment of the buyer and the buyer's particular situations. It may be possible to be less severe if much business has been done before and the way of working established.

In many cases contract negotiations are dictated by the company's own manner of working. Documentation is a good example of this. Many good engineering companies produce excellent products, that work properly, on time but the documentation that should come with the equipment is often late and incomplete. Because of this experience the firm itself is careful to avoid any penalty on late documentation being written into any contract especially overseas. This reduces the ability of the negotiator to move easily on this point when the problem could probably be easily overcome by an alteration in the firm's management of documentation.

Many of the policies of the supplier will have been built up over the years and may seriously affect negotiations: we will never do this or that sort of project; we cannot compete in that market; export is not for us; we cannot get the labour, etc, etc,—these policies may have had good foundation once but it is wise for companies to shake the skeletons out of the cupboards occasionally otherwise valuable markets may be left to some enterprising competitors.

While in this chapter there are several sections closely integrated to one another, this "ability to negotiate" is in a sense an overview of the others as they stem from an examination of this question. We go on now to look at what may be at the grass roots of the ability to negotiate.

## 14:5  COMPANY FACILITIES AND RESOURCES

It is educational for all companies to look at their facilities and resources from the point of view of the buyer and what the buyer really wants. The buyer wants his goods on time, to the specification and guaranteed trouble free for a particular period. How many companies, and that means the managers, project managers and others associated with the company business, seriously take time off to study what is, after all, a reasonable requirement?

For example, there are still large numbers of firms that have no efficient progressing system or project management as an integral part of their projects. For many firms quality control is something you do at the end "to see if everything is all right." Many others know this is absurd and that quality control starts at the beginning of a project and has to be managed right through. This includes adequate subsystems tests so that one has an exceedingly low probability of getting to the end of the project only to find the final item does not perform to specification. All these measures if properly applied can:

1    Ensure a timely product
2    Give a product that works properly
3    Make the reliability adequate for the purpose

This is not only what a buyer wants but it gives the supplier the confidence he wants in order to tender for a project and win.

## 14:6  SUBCONTRACTED ITEMS AND
## FINANCING OF SUBCONTRACTORS

Although we deal with subcontracting in Chapter 15, the payment of subcontractors, contingency against failure and cash-flow problems can affect the tender price.

There is first the question of mark up: what percentage if any is to be applied to the subcontractor's price? There may be technical risk in that deficiencies in performance will have to be made good. Is there any risk that the subcontractor will fail and a more expensive substitute have to be found? Payment to the subcontractor may be made at different times to the expected input of money from the customer and this means, effectively, that the main contractor is financing the subcontractor, if only for short periods. This incurs interest charges that may be incorporated into the price to the customer or preferably avoided altogether by different arrangements.

## 14:7  CASH-FLOW COSTS

In determining the price an important factor to bear in mind is the effect of the payment conditions attached to the contract, on the cash flow. To take the most obvious case. Suppose the contract is worth £100000 and no payment is received until the end then for the project duration the company is increasingly out of pocket. To support the project activities the company has to pay out of its own resources. This costs money either in real interest charges or in charges set against the project in view of the fact that the money cannot be used elsewhere.

A worse position that has beset many a company is running out of money, not being able to borrow any and going bankrupt or ending up in a very difficult position. This case of no money until the end on a large project is not only bad for the supplier but may be equally bad for the buyer because of the risks mentioned above. On the other hand, it is unreasonable to expect the buyer to pay all before the contract is complete. One arrangement is a deposit on signing the contract followed by progress payments. It is the amount of the deposit and the relationship of the progress payments against the actual money spent by the supplier that determines the cash flow. The easiest way to get a first shot at the cash flow effects is to assume that say 10% interest will be paid on money outstanding and say 7% on money surpluses. For ease of calculation, assume step functions for money flows rather than a variable line, for example:

| | | |
|---|---|---|
| Payment condition is: | 10% | contract signing |
| | 80% | 1 year later |
| | 10% | 1 year later |
| Total contract value of | 100% = say £100000 | |
| Expenditure is: | £40000 at 3 months from signing | |
| | £60000 at 1 year from signing | |
| Total | £100000 | |

As there is assumed to be no expenditure for 3 months the £10 000 deposit earns $10\,000 \times \frac{3}{12} \times \frac{7}{100}$ interest = £175 (credit) (assuming 7% interest received). The £40 000 expenditure has a £10 000 deposit to set against it thus we have £30 000 outstanding for 9 months. This equals $30\,000 \times \frac{10}{100} \times \frac{9}{12}$ = £2222 (debit) (assuming 10% paid).

At one year a further payment of £80000 is made but expenditure is

£60000. There is also a debit of £30000 existing. The balance is a debit of
£10000 for the second year. This equals interest of £1000 (debit).

At the end of the second year the debit balance of £10000 is extinguished
by the final payment of 10% or £10000.

The total interest position due to this particular cash flow is thus £3222
debit and £175 credit. With these payment terms the company thus loses
£3047. (Profit elements in the money have been ignored for the example.)

If the contract value were double, the losses double. It is clear that on any
large contract the effect of timing of cash flows could be serious.

There are further refinements that we could be made to the calculations
but they would be of a second order effect. We therefore suggest that the
simple method outlined will suffice in most cases.

## 14:8  COMMISSIONS, FEES AND BONUSES

While the bulk of the expenses associated with the tender preparation will
probably be covered by the overheads structure in the company finances
there are occasionally certain fees and commissions that may have to be paid
for consultancy, introduction of business and bonuses for special services
rendered. All this is a cost against the project and must be properly included
otherwise any overall discount given later on the accumulated price is based
on a false premise. As with all the other expenses the golden rule is knowledge of them, inclusion in the tender costs, and then a deliberate consideration if a discount is to be applied.

## 14:9  FINANCING CHARGES

We have mentioned subcontracting and charges, but the charges we now
come to could be more serious. We have also mentioned the effects of timing
of cash flows and these effectively give rise to charges for finance. However,
another set of charges may arise if the supplier (or other body) positively
finances the customer. Invariably the supplier does not do this directly but
through a third party, nearly always a bank. In overseas countries, especially,
lines of credit have to be established when insufficient of the sellers currency
is available due to the trade balance of payments position. The buyer is liable
through his bank and the seller through the bank creating the line of credit
for finance charges. Coupled with this will be charges from ECGD for
backing the loan.

On other occasions the particular contract may be difficult for normal
stock bank procedures and a specialist finance house has to be called in to
arrange the deal. In this case it is likely that the charges for the service

will increase. The seller therefore will have to include in his overhead costs a figure of around 3% to cover bank loan charges and ECGD cover. (This figure has to be checked at the time as interest rates vary.)

## 14:10 NEGOTIATING MARGINS

This very much depends on whether there is the opportunity for negotiation. If the tender has to be submitted in a sealed envelope and then later the successful firm is notified yes or no, there is not much scope for real negotiation.

In dealing with many buying agencies, especially in Eastern Europe, there is nearly always the chance to negotiate in person. Knowledge of what margin can either be built in for the purpose or more than given away (then virtually a discount) is obviously very important. The use of this margin should be as far as possible *quid pro quo* against, say, commercial conditions unless the supplier feels he wants the work urgently, and then it will be a discount anyway.

## 14:11 CONTINGENCY

This is a straightforward reserve in the price after assessment of risks and any penalties that might arise in carrying out the project. It is again, what the project price can carry and is dependent upon how much the contract is wanted. If the contingencies are judged to be really needed then it is perhaps better for the job to be lost than remove them. It is a matter of very fine judgement.

## 14:12 TURNKEY PROJECTS—PROJECT MANAGEMENT

In a project where a project manager (and perhaps staff) is required, then costs will be incurred. These will have to be built into the price or given away knowingly. It is unfortunately rarer than it should be that the customer acknowledges the cost and is willing to pay for it. Many customers know it must happen, but few accept that the service should be costed separately. As long as the cost is hidden and the total price still competitive, that is all that seems to be required. In fact on a large contract the customer will be much more secure where a proper project management structure has been set up by one supplier than if another supplier is a little cheaper but has a weaker organisation.

On turnkey projects one could argue that the question does not matter as the supplier is totally responsible for the complete implementation and anything that is wrong has to be put right by him. However, it is likely that it is vital for the customer to receive the completed project on time and a better organised supplier with clear management aims in the management of the project although more expensive may overall be cheaper in the end if delays and lack of management can embarrass the customer.

All this means that project management costs money, but it can also save money in the long run. However, it does not always follow that the cheaper tender cannot employ project management. Costs may have been cut elsewhere. In presenting a tender to a customer it is essential to be aware of how to present the project management case. The customer may ask for it, in which case competition is even. If it is not asked for, should one emphasise it or not. To answer the question it is necessary to know the job, the customer and the circumstances. The sure fact is that the management of projects in general is considerably underrated.

## 14:13  COMPENSATING TRADING

In Eastern European projects, where foreign currency is short, there will often be a demand for compensation trading. This is a contracted obligation by the supplier to purchase goods from the customer's country to a certain percentage value of the contract price, perhaps 50%. As it is rare for the supplier to have such buying and, more important, such selling facilities, there are specialist firms that will arrange to buy the goods and charge the supplier a fee for doing so. The fee may be up to 20% of the value of the goods purchased, but typically 15%. However, the supplier not the third party has to contract with the customer. This is how it would work:

| | |
|---|---:|
| Contract value (say) | £500 000 |
| Compensation trading asked for, (negotiation obviously is called for) is 40%, i.e. | £200 000 |
| Fee for specialist firm (which guarantees to buy from customers country £200 000 worth of goods) say 15% = | £30 000 |

The supplier then has to decide in the light of competition whether to absorb or charge the £30 000 or partially absorb it. There is probably no particular need to absorb it as the buyer knows it costs a supplier to carry out compensation trading. The benefit to the buyer is £200 000 worth of foreign currency towards the project costs. However, as always, the decision is with the supplier and how badly he wants the work.

There is usually included in the compensation trading agreement, a penalty clause such that if the supplier does not buy either the correct mix of goods (previously arranged in the contract), the total value of goods contracted for, or purchase within a given time, then a penalty has to be paid on the balance of the goods value not yet purchased. This could be 10 to 15%, but is negotiable. Obviously the supplier has to enter into a contract with the third party that is doing the actual buying, and any risk of paying penalties included in the tender price structure. Usually the third party will indemnify the supplier against such penalties.

## 14:14 BANK GUARANTEES

Some customers want a bank guarantee against any deposit or down payment they may have paid before the arrival of any goods from the supplier. For example, if 5% down payment has been paid on contract signing, the customer may want the supplier to sign a bank guarantee so that if the goods do not arrive at the right time, the customer may automatically get from the supplier's bank the 5% payment.

In most cases this arrangement is sensible and will not be used unless the supplier is obviously not able to fulfil his part of the bargain. In other cases especially where deliveries are several and made over a period, the use of the bank guarantee can get complicated. As far as the cost of it is concerned, as distinct from the overall commercial considerations, it is normally a small item measured in hundreds of pounds rather than thousands. Typically the percentage figure charge on the amount involved would be 10% on a project of £500 000 and a 5% down payment (or £25 000); the charge by the bank would thus be £250.

## 14:15 LIQUIDATED DAMAGES

As, in general terms, there is no such thing as a "penalty" in English Law, contracts write in a section dealing with liquidated damages. This is a prescribed amount of money or percentage of the contract price payable on non-delivery of the product or system or achievement of the project. It is usually tied to time such that the damages accumulate in value the longer the non-delivery or similar fault remains.

Companies are often involved in trade-off calculations of damages against cost of speeding up work. The damages are "liquidated" because they have a maximum and are normally in lieu of any other damages except breach of contract. In tendering, great care should be exercised in assessing truthfully the real chance of adhering faithfully to delivery dates in view of any liquidated damages and their amount in the contract.

## 14:16  DISCOUNTS OR PRICE CUTTING

While in a different category from the other factors that have been considered in price construction, discounts have an obviously special place in setting the final price. If all the other factors mentioned are properly calculated, then a discount can be more scientifically applied, if required, in the knowledge that one is not plunging into the unknown. At least a discount can then be fully recognisable for what it is and due account may be taken of it in the accounting system rather than a lot of unseen chipping away of profits. Whether a discount should be given is a complex question. It depends on conditions such as whether:

1    The company is desperate for work
2    The contract is a strategic one that will lead to other work
3    An arrangement exists—for example, with a large buyer in the private
     or public sector

# 15

# Subcontractors

Many organisations, faced with the decision to implement a new project decide to place the whole work of project implementation with one main contrator. This has clear advantages, particularly for those organisations with little or no experience of project management. Paradoxically, it is quite often the experienced organisation that delegates the whole project to one main contractor, while the inexperienced go blithely ahead to manage their own project.

There are advantages to a customer in having to deal with only one main contractor. There is a clear point at which the customer can apply pressure, and he is relieved of the problem of resolving disputes between subcontractors. In a complex project for instance, it is sometimes extremely difficult to diagnose the cause of a fault and, hence, when there are many subcontractors, it is equally difficult to decide which subcontractor is responsible for rectifying the fault. Anyone with experience of going live with a new complex computer project knows the problem of trying to isolate a fault, which may be due to hardware, software, application program, communication line, straight operator error, or indeed a mixture of these. A fault which clearly appears to be hardware may, after lengthy investigation, prove to be software. Similar problems arise in other advanced technology fields. Unless the customer has given open-ended cost plus contracts to his subcontractors or unless he is very experienced in project management, he is better to pass the problem of resolving these disputes to a contractor.

Whether project management is carried out directly by the sponsoring organisation or by a main contractor, the project manager will be conerned with the following problems related to subcontractors:

1    The decision on what work to do "in house" and what work to subcontract
2    The organisation into packages of the work to be subcontracted
3    The choice of subcontractors
4    The contract with subcontractors
5    The day-to-day control of progress and quality

## 15:1  WHAT TO SUBCONTRACT

In the first planning stage, the project manager will have identified the major activities, which will go to make up the project. These should now be examined with a view to deciding which activities have to be subcontracted and which should be done "in house." Many different factors enter into this decision. The overriding one—certainly for a main contractor handling a project—is whether it will be more profitable for him to subcontract or not. Whether or not it is more profitable, of course, depends upon whether the work is done efficiently.

The first consideration for the PM will be whether the resources, of the right quality, will be available to him at the right time. If they will be, then, in the absence of special circumstances, he is likely to have the work done in house. However, in many cases, the resources will not be available and a decision then has to be made whether the company should acquire the resources to make them available for this project, or whether the work should be subcontracted. The actual decision will be made in most cases by senior management, but the project manager may be able to influence it and should certainly understand the factors involved.

The company may have evolved a general policy in connection with subcontracting. It may, for instance, have decided that there are certain areas that lie outside its main business. Whenever the company is involved in work in that area it will subcontract the work. There may even be agreements with other companies such that all work in a particular field will always be offered to ABC company in return for certain special trading benefits. The company's normal level of operation also affects the position. It may be policy to maintain the company's resources at a uniformly high level of utilisation and subcontract any extra work, unless there is a clear expectation that the load will continue for the foreseeable future.

It may be that some part of the project requires special skills, knowledge or equipment that is not available in the company. Unless there is expected

to be continuity of employment or unless the project provides the opportunity of extending its activities into this new area, it will normally be
necessary to subcontract. There are, of course, some hazards in subcontracting because one does not have the specialist skills or knowledge. It does
mean that one may have to rely on an outside firm for some activity that is
vital to the success of the project. In these circumstances one has to be
particularly careful to ensure that one picks a subcontractor that will neither
let one down nor take one for a ride.

With many large projects there may be a desire to involve local interests
in order to obtain and maintain local goodwill. This is particularly so in the
case of large construction or mining projects in remote places. The local
economy may well be dislocated by the project and involving local subcontractors may help to get at least some of the local people on your side.
This is just as true of projects in the remoter areas of Britain as it is of
distant countries. There may also be some cost benefits in using local subcontractors, though their lower wage rates may be offset by lower productivity. A further advantage in using local subcontractors on overseas projects
is that the project demands on the customer for scarce foreign currency may
be kept down. This is likely to be a particular advantage in any project being
executed in a country with current balance of payments difficulties. Many
developing countries like some subcontracts placed locally so that there is
a spin-off in know-how for local firms.

In Western Europe an appreciable number of large projects are commiss-
ioned by international organisations. In these cases the original decision
on the main contractor is taken by a head count of the representatives of
the various nations forming the organisation. Here the main contractor may
well try to gather a collection of subcontractors from the various countries
concerned in order to try to influence the order. It sometimes happens in
such cases that a consortium of firms is formed to go for the order. The final
form of the consortium may be that one firm becomes main contractor for
the project while the others become subcontractors to the main contractor.
In all these cases the decisions on subcontracting are made in order to get
the order in the first place and the project manager is stuck with them.

In all cases where the project manager has any control over whether or not
to subcontract, he should try to put the test: "Will it be more profitable, if
I subcontract this work?" In making this choice he will obviously have to
consider whether there is a suitable and reliable subcontractor. However,
before he comes to the question of choice of subcontractor, the project
manager should consider how the work should be packaged for subcontracting.

In large construction projects it is not unknown for several hundred subcontractors to be involved on the same project. This can be an extremely difficult situation to control as delays by one subcontractor can and probably will affect several others. Quite a large and energetic project team is needed just to keep track of the subcontractors' progress and to sort out the continuous sqabbling over who is to blame for what. There is a great deal to be said in such cases for grouping the work into about six main sectors and putting these out to main subcontractors leaving them the headache of keeping their team of subcontractors in step. They will, of course, charge something for their trouble and for, in effect, providing a small project team but the same management principle of limiting the span of control applies as it does in the normal line management situation.

When there are a hundred different subcontractors working on activities, which interact with each other, there is a lot more to controlling them and keeping them in step, than just running your PERT through a computer. The computer helps, of course, but there is still the problem of reconciling the many conflicting interests and in most cases also dealing with some incompatabilities between people.

Once the packages to be subcontracted have been decided upon, there is the problem of choice of the subcontrators. In most companies there will be a part of the company, perhaps a commercial department, that will be concerned with the mechanics of inviting tenders. The project manager will however be concerned with defining that which is to be tendered for and also with the evaluation of the tenders. He may also be allowed some say in deciding which firms should be invited to tender.

The definition of the work to be done is a tricky task, particularly as the time and resources available for doing it are most often much less than is really needed. The work has to be well enough defined, first, so that the tenderers have a sufficiently clear picture of what is required of them so that they can determine whether they have the resources needed and can quote a realistic price, to which they can be held. The second reason is that there should be enough information for the main contractor to estimate a "standard" price for the job, against which the actual tenders can be judged. This is particularly important if there is any likelihood of the companies tendering forming a ring to keep prices up.

As well as defining the more obvious tasks, it it necessary to consider whether and to what extent documentation will be required from the subcontractor and what supporting or continuing services will be needed. If there will be constraints on the subcontractors work, these must be spelt out. He may well, for instance, be allowed access to site only at certain times. His work will have to interlock with other project activities. All this will affect his price.

Some companies have approved lists of subcontractors. They may regularly subcontract all work of a certain kind to perhaps two or three firms and try to keep a balance between them. In some cases they may even give all work of one kind to a particular firm. In such a case, if trust and goodwill have been built up between the firms over several projects, it may be possible to short-circuit some of the definition in the early stages. The sanction of the possible loss of future business can be a powerful one. However, it is not an excuse for the project manager to be slack. If he is slack in defining the work, or later in controlling it, at best there will be expensive misunderstandings; At worst the subcontractor will take advantage of him.

## 15:2 TENDERS AND CHOOSING SUBCONTRACTORS

If tenders are invited from several firms, a most important task for the project manager is helping to evaluate the tenders. Once the tenders have been received they must be examined, first to see whether they represent a viable proposal. This will probably involve him in meetings with several of the tenderers to clarify points in their tenders.

Where such clarification is obtained and the tender is still being seriously considered, the additional facts undertakings or clarification should be committed to writing and agreed by the tenderer in writing.

It is important in comparing tenders, to compare them on a basis that is truly comparable. Like must be compared with like. It is very difficult to compare the true cost of a machine that carries an absolute guarantee and free maintenance for six months with one which carries the same guarantee for two years. The way in which the invitation to tender is expressed will help to ensure comparable tenders. The more specific and clear you can be in defining your requirements, the more likely you are to obtain comparable tenders. When there are several tenders it probably pays, as part of the evaluation, to prepare a tabulation of the key features of the tenders. In particular the prices that are to be compared must be for comparable contracts.

Sometimes when the prices are compared, one contractor stands out from the rest either because his price is very much lower or very much higher than the rest. A very low price may mean that the tenderer's costs are low and he can genuinely offer a lower price. He may have natural advantages, arising from location, sources of supply or a reliable work force. He may have greater productivity than his competitors as a result of better management and appropriate capital equipment. He may have a better understanding of the work to be done than his competitors and perhaps better than yours. This may mean that he can see geniune short cuts to producing what you really need. He may need the work because his order book is not full and he has underused resources, which makes him willing to cut his profit margins. At the extreme, he may be in severe difficulties and deliberately not only forego his profit margin but also ignore his overheads and cost on a marginal costing basis. From the project manager's point of view all these reasons may be acceptable, so long as he can be sure that the firm will survive to deliver the goods.

Another reason for a low quote may, however, be a failure to understand fully what is required. Similarly, a low quote may be due to a rushed and less than competently produced tender. A fairly simple arithmetic error in a key calculation can result in a cost that is as low as half what it should be. Either of these reasons, combined with marginal costing or survival difficulties can lead you forward to disaster.

It is well known in many industries that if an initial order can be obtained on a low price quotation, the profit on the job can be obtained from changes to specification by extras or by straight price increases as the work proceeds. To avoid this some firms try to obtain fixed price offers from their sub-contractors. There is one well documented case of a major oil refinery construction project. The main contractor lined up his subcontractors before he put his own tender in. He managed to obtain a very low fixed-price tender for a vital and large part of the work. This low price was a significant element in the main contractor's own costing. Shortly afterwards the subcontractor went into liquidation. The main contractor had to get a replacement subcontractor in a hurry. He found himself committed to "what proved to be a highly unfavourable and virtually open-ended subcontract from which stems most of the anguish suffered. . . ." A very substantial loss was made on the project, although this was not the only reason for loss.

When a very low price is quoted for a subcontract it pays to ask the question "why?" and to make sure that you get a convincing and reassuring answer. One of the astronauts on an Appollo mission is quoted as saying: "It is a sobering thought that one is going on a journey of millions of miles into space, carried by a vehicle made up of over a million parts, each one of which has been selected on the basis of the lowest tender."

A very high price must also be considered critically. It may be quoted because the contractor's costs are higher than his competitors. It may be that his quality control and standards of workmanship are higher and that this is reflected in his costs. It may be that he does not particularly want the work and has tendered in a fairly cursory way, making sure that any gaps in his calculations were covered by high contingencies. He may even have gone to the lengths of deliberately quoting an outrageously high price because although he doesn't want the job, he does not want to be seen not to tender.

There is, however, another possible reason for an apparently very high price. It may be that this firm really understands what is required and has costed the job on the basis of the real requirements, while its competitors have overlooked some of the costly aspects of the job. If this proves to be so, then the other tenderers have to be cross-examined very carefully to bring the contents of their tenders into line.

When it finally comes to choosing the subcontractor from among several contenders, what are the key factors that must be taken into account? The prime criterion for selection is: "Will he stay in business and do a technically sound job on time?" In considering the tenders you must consider whether the tenderer is indeed capable of doing a technically sound job. Has he staff with the required knowledge and skills? Does he have the necessary plant and equipment? Is his management competent to control the work, to obtain the necessary quality standards and to get the work done on time? Is the firm one that has a reputation for honouring its commitments? If not, it should not have been invited to tender in the first place. It is extremely important to satisfy yourself that the firm is sound and likely to stay in business. Even if the subcontract is for a comparatively small amount of work, costing a fairly small sum, the consequences of failure can be severe.

Finding a replacement contractor at short notice may be both difficult and expensive. The effect of delay on the work of the other subcontractors may be expensive. Completion of the project may be delayed with all the inevitable effects on overrun costs and possibly penalties to be borne. It is quite possible for the costs resulting from the failure of a small subcontractor to run into many times—may be even a hundred times—the value of the original subcontract. The point is that the lowest tendered price does not always result in the lowest actual cost. Although price, clearly, cannot be disregarded, the lowest priced tender should not automatically and uncritically be accepted.

In some spheres it is common practice not only to go for lowest prices, but to try to beat down the selected subcontractor to an absolutely rock bottom price. This generally proves an unsatisfactory arrangement as the subcontractor is subsequently mainly concerned with avoiding his contract and concentrating his real efforts on other and more profitable contracts. If you allow your subcontractor to make a fair profit you are more likely to obtain co-operation from him and to get results from him.

## 15:3 SUBCONTRACTS—POINTS TO WATCH

When you enter into a contract with your subcontractor it is essential, once again, to ensure that the contract is as clear as possible about what is to be done by the subcontractor. It is necessary to be quite clear about what the price covers and about what the subcontractor is committed to doing, but may charge extra for. It may be useful to mention some of the troublesome areas we have come across:

**1** *Documentation.* How much is to be provided and in what detail? Is it to be merely sufficient for user needs or should it be sufficiently detailed to cover the needs of maintenance engineers? How many copies are to be provided and at what stage in the project? Is the documentation to be in English or is it required in a different language?

**2** *Test equipment and spares.* Are the essential items to be provided by the subcontractor in the price or do you have to procure separately?

**3** *Acceptance testing.* Does the price allow for the costs involved in formal acceptance tests, witnessed by you or by the final customer? For government contracts a whole series of acceptance tests may be a requirement of the main contract.

**4** *Technical support.* Will the subcontractor supply support in your factory or on the project site and on what terms? As the project is run up prior to going live a good deal of on-site support may be required. After "go live" some backing high-quality technical support may be needed for the regular maintenance force.

**5** *Actual delivery date or dates.* It is essential to have a schedule of these. For newly developed equipment, for instance, you may require a pilot delivery for exhaustive testing. Is the cost of bringing the pilot delivery items up to the final production standard included in the price or not?

Perhaps the most important aspect of a subcontract is that it must be kept in line with the main contract for the project. It is an extremely tricky business to keep them in line as the main contractor normally has to have a fairly firm arrangement with his subcontractors before he puts his own tender in. For government projects there may well be a lot of small print clauses or conditions that have to be passed on. Matters relating to guarantees, insurance and liabilities must, of course, be kept in line. It may not be quite so obvious, but where there are many subcontractors, they interact with each other as well as with the main contractor and so the various subcontracts have to be kept in line with each other in the appropriate places.

## 15:4   SUBCONTRACT PROGRESSING

To carry this out successfully, it is necessary to have a detailed plan from the subcontractor, including a network of his activities. There should be an agreed list of important events or milestones. These include dates for such things as delivery, start of acceptance test and completion of important intermediate events.

Arrangements should be made to have the maximum possible visibility of the subcontractor's work. If the work is being done in his factory you should consider having a quality man in his factory or regular visits by a progress chaser. Similarly, if the work is done on site there should be provision for checking on the quality of work and its progress against schedule.

However, one does not keep a dog and bark oneself. The subcontractor is told what is required of him and when. So far as possible the "how" should be left to him.

## 15:5   LABOUR AND CONSTRUCTION PROJECTS

Large construction projects are susceptible to one particular form of trouble caused by the employment of several subcontractors. Men from many different firms find themselves on site at the same time and subject to the same site difficulties. They talk together, both at work and off duty in the local pubs. If they discover that Mr *A*, working for one firm, and Mr *B*, working for another firm, are being paid different rates, work different hours and get different rates of expenses, there will be trouble—particularly if the men belong to the same union. One large firm in Britain tackles this in a way that is effective but takes a lot of skilled effort and negotiation. It imposes labour conditions for the project on all its subcontractors, which it has agreed individually with the unions concerned.

## 15:6   SUCCESSFUL SUBCONTRACTING

All aspects of a project are interlinked. Failure by one subcontractor may lead through a long chain of events to serious problems for the main contractor and for the project. When employing subcontractors it is essential to select those you can trust to stay in business and do a sound technical job on time. It is essential to specify clearly to the subcontractor what is required of him. The corollary of this is that all specification changes must be agreed and carefully documented.

It is essential to require an effective standard of performance from subcontractors. If they show any sign of falling down on the job they must be chased very hard at the correct management level.

Subcontractors, if they are to perform well must be treated fairly. We must scrupulously avoid blaming them to the customer for anything that goes wrong that was our fault. It rarely pays to drive too hard a bargain with a subcontractor. If the price is pared right down, it is certain the standard

of service and of quality will also be pared down. Any subcontractor should
be allowed, indeed encouraged, to make a fair profit from the project. This
will help to provide him with an incentive to play his part in attaining your
objective—a successful project.

# 16

# The Contract

For many projects, there is one main contractor, responsible to the customer for the execution of the project. In such cases there will be a contract between the two parties, setting out their respective obligations. In most companies, the project manager appointed by the contractor will not be responsible for the contract negotiations. This will be the responsibility of the legal or contracts department or possibly of the company secretary. Nonetheless, the contract is a document of crucial interest to the project manager. He must be fully aware of the contents of the contract.

## 16:1  PROJECT MANAGER INVOLVEMENT

The project manager should be involved in discussions leading up to a contract for several reasons. The discharge of the contract normally comes when implementation of the project is complete except for some maintenance obligations that might exist. Completion of implementation is largely, if not entirely, dictated by some sort of acceptance test or takeover procedure. This in turn is the climax of the project manager's work. He should certainly have a voice in that climax by being involved at an early stage in the contractual negotiations.

There will be other items, such as delivery and intermediate tests, that will be of importance to him. Problems may arise in these circumstances between the salesman, the contract department and the project manager. If the project manager has had the right job and formal training he should be able to work with salesmen and know how to help without appearing to be obstructive. The salesman for his part must learn to accept the project manager for what he is and have confidence that by working together he can move on to the next sale that much more quickly; if bonus is involved, this means the salesman can earn more money. In some companies the project manager is not appointed until a contract is signed; in these circumstances the project manager must read the contract very carefully and any items that he feels is unsatisfactory should be communicated to the management without delay, preferably with some recommendation about what the company can now do.

When several people in a company are concerned with a contract, it is essential that they are clear between them on who is to do the contractual negotiation with the customer. In our experience this has normally been the contracts department. All letters, relating to the contract, go from this one man. He sends copies of all the letters he sends and receives, to both the salesman and the project manager. If the project manager intends to send a letter to the customer and feels it may have contractual implications, he should let the contracts department have a look at the draft. Needless to say, if such a system is to work, the draft has to be cleared promptly. The project manager himself must keep a copy of the contract with the files of contract correspondence, indexed in such a way that he can turn up important letters quickly.

## 16:2  BASIC RULES

There are a few basic rules about contracts that project managers should understand, although we make no pretence that what we write is any treatise on the law of contract. For a contract to be binding upon the parties and, perhaps more important, enforceable at law, six requirements have to exist:

1   The contract must not set out to do anything unlawful.
2   The parties constructing a contract must be able to make such a contract. An obvious case of someone unable to make a contract would be a party that is insolvent. A less obvious case, and probably not common, is when the memorandum of articles of a company does not at the time permit it to enter into a particular contract.
3   The parties must have intended to enter into a contract. For example, hints and tips that one party will do something for another are not a sound basis for the other party to rely on if the matter concerned some long-term arrangement. It is far better to have a contract if the backing of the law may be.required.
4   A contract cannot be one-sided. If there is an offer by someone to do

something or supply something, then equally there must be an acceptance
by the other party that he agrees to have the goods or the task carried out.
5    What the law calls "consideration" must be involved—that is, something
of value must be given in exchange for the supply of the goods or services.
Whatever it is, it has to be something definite and of value.
6    The final point is that the contract must not be invalidated by a genuine
mistake. This is clearly a tricky area and requires expert advice; suffice it to
say here that the sort of thing that might apply is a mistake as to the identity
of the subject matter of the contract or a mistake as to the existence of facts
that may form the basis of the contract. However, this is an area where the
utmost caution is required from non-legal persons and, we understand, some
reasonable caution from lawyers themselves.

## 16:3    ACCEPTANCE TESTS

This is an area where the project manager should know intimately what has
been arranged so that he can ensure the best chance of success. Unless the
project is simple there is almost sure to be some new angle on the final
result that has a bearing on the acceptance test and how it was set up in the
first place.

It is essential to agree on the criteria by which the tests are to be judged
successful or otherwise. It is essential to have tests that are realistic and
which it is practicable to carry out. The impact of the tests on changes in the
requirements must be watched as the project progresses.

It may be that the customer has altered his use of the equipment even in
some small way. The previous agreement must now of necessity be reconsi-
dered in the light of this new information. The project manager has the
highest chance of achieving a satisfactory result if he is steeped in this aspect
from the very beginning, talking to the customer and helping to formulate the
tests.

## 16:4    PENALTIES

Another item that will occupy his attention, if it is included in the contract,
is any form of penalty. This comes more correctly under the heading of
*liquidated damages*, where prescribed sums of money can be extracted from
the supplier in the event of lateness or non-performance of various kinds.

The project manager must ensure that his project does not result in the
payment of penalties and therefore must thoroughly understand the penalty
situation. The penalty for lateness is the simplest and typical case. The
project manager may have to trade-off or balance resources of one kind or

another. First, however, is the burden of proof. If the customer has caused some lateness himself the regular meetings already mentioned previously must be the vehicle for ironing out the real responsibilities. With proof comes confidence and with confidence usually comes, perhaps paradoxically, an amicable settlement.

The picture here is not some hole-in-the-corner, catch-you-if-I-can, attitude but a mature businesslike approach to the essential job of establishing responsibilities and accountability. In the matter of trade-offs it has to be decided, for instance, how much money can be spent to plug a particular penalty gap. Should one spend £10 000 to save £5000? In many cases the answer must be no, but it depends on what that delay is costing the customer and how far one is to be concerned about it. In the majority of cases suppliers do try, penalty or not, to satisfy the customer. The reasons are simple. First, simple moral considerations may influence some companies to avoid lateness and pay the excess themselves. This is not as rare a virtue as one might think. Second, bad news travels fast and if the supplier is doing a bad job it gets around in that industry and competitors will make the most of it. It is another trade-off consideration that £5000 inbalance seen above may be as nothing compared with the damage that piece of bad business could do. The project manager must investigate the various trade-off positions and, perhaps with higher management assistance in some cases, decide on the relevant actions and expenditure of resources.

## 16:5   SERVICEABILITY

While not all projects include serviceability criteria, many will. This is a fairly complex issue. It is not just a case of how often a piece of equipment can fail, e.g., not more than once a month. It is also necessary to consider the question of how long the item can fail for. It may be all right to fail for an hour a month or half an hour a fortnight.

Even as simple a case as this can cause trouble. How do you define a fortnight? Is it any two consecutive weeks? Does any one week form a part of two different fortnights? Simple plain English definitions must be examined closely to see that there is no possibility of ambiguity.

The time out of service is every bit as important as the time between failures. If, for example, a project manager cannot ensure that the intrinsic reliability of a piece of equipment is improved sufficiently to meet basic reliability figures, he may make it acceptable by improving the recovery time to make the item fully serviceable again. This may mean expenditure on maintenance but may avoid a difficult contractual situation.

## 16:6  DOCUMENTATION

Often there are quite large quantities of written material on the use, care and maintenance of the equipment and the supply of this documentation is usually covered in the contract. It is invariably a long-delivery item and by its nature is subject to change and, hence, delays. It will be on the macro-net but certainly, from the experience of many project managers, it is worth watching closely. If it does look as though trouble is brewing it may be possible to alleviate it by interim documentation. This may not look so well turned out as the final documents ought to be, but could stop a little argument growing into a catastrophe. One must try to prevent the customer from getting into a position where arguments can occur. With documentation the position is part emotional, as the intrinsic value is small, but part, of course, could be really critical for the customer in having to carry out tasks on the project without the knowledge that the documentation could give.

Documentation is often treated with a certain amount of contempt, the "we can soon get a few manuals together" type of attitude. It does take a long time to prepare certain documentation, the updating is tedious and vital and, unless well planned and progressed, can soon cause problems. Some companies feel that documentation is critical enough to have liquidated damages with it, hence its possible contractual importance.

## 16:7  ADVICE AND COUNSEL

While not likely to be missed in the contractual negotiations the exact interpretation of responsibility over advice and counsel can be difficult because of the probability of greater project knowledge by the supplier. It is expected that this knowledge exists. Helpful advice without clarity of responsibility has sometimes rebounded. Don't stop the advice, get the accountability right.

## 16:8  TRAINING AND SERVICE

On many projects the customer has to take over the project when it is complete and operate it—for example, a computer, an engineering project, a ship, an aeroplane, etc. In this "taking over" the supplier will have often had to train the customer staff in the operation and/or maintenance of a whole or part of the project. This may involve many different categories of staff and types of training. It is not always possible, especially in projects where the customer is very much involved, to state precisely beforehand what amount of training and other items the customer will ultimately require. Sometimes a block figure is put in the contract to cover it, or a "rate per hour" type of approach is used or a combination of both. It is important to get the whole arrangement very clear otherwise misunderstandings on what has actually been promised can easily occur.

This problem is accentuated in Eastern Europe where, in order to save foreign currency, the customer often wishes to do as much of the work as possible. This brings us to the next contractual issue, often a major one.

## 16:9 PROJECT RESPONSIBILITY

When a supplier makes something and hands it to a customer who uses it properly the responsibility is clear in that some sort of warranty will cover the situation afterwards. Many projects are of this nature. Some projects, especially in the engineering field, by their very nature involve an interface with customer equipment so that a joint responsibility exists. However, customers generally like the supplier to assume responsibility and so not only has one got a general task requirement specification but also an interface specification.

One example of such a case could be the supply of a computer to control an electricity undertaking where control work is undertaken by the computer and the communications to and from the computer is provided by the customer. Both supplier and customer are interlinked—either can fail the other. Who is totally responsible? Should the supplier take on the total responsibility after the communication interfaces have been defined? Is this risk to be put in terms of extra money? When such a project as this is set up it is clear that the project manager must watch the responsibilities very closely because of the close ties between customer and supplier.

## 16:10 CUSTOMER RELATIONS

In general terms the contract by definition must set down the supplier/user relationship as far as the law is concerned. An aspect of project management that we are keen on for reasons that we hope are quite logical is to try to prevent the customer from getting in a position where arguments can occur.

It is not possible for the project manager to look completely after the customer's interests but we believe that this aspect is important. If the project manager can see a way in which the customer will make a mistake, tell him, try to help him. Nearly all contractual problems, apart from sheer obvious cases of breach, arise from a lack of clarity and hence a difference of opinion. Contractual definition must follow the same rules as the technical definition. If packing and shipment are involved do not let simple administration mistakes turn into acrimony. The project manager should sit heavily on such matters because he knows what can happen when these things go wrong.

The project manager has a diplomatic task on his hands when the user does not use the equipment as it is supposed to be used. This is likely to invalidate guarantees and can cause much friction. The user must be educated back to correct usage before the damage is done. This sort of problem includes environmental conditions if they are applicable.

# Part Six

# SUMMARY

# 17

# Project Success

What does one mean when one talks of project success? At the simplest, it may be said that a project is successful if it meets its project aims in terms of cost, time and performance. This presupposes that the original project evaluation was a sound one. It also presupposes that the project aim was sound. A hotel group might decide to build a new motel at Little Backwater on Marsh. The basis of the decision might be that Britain's entry into the EEC is about to turn Little Backwater into an important communications centre. The project may be completed on time and within budget. The group may be satisfied that performance specifications have been met. The finish and workmanship is excellent. The project manager hands over to the hotel manager. Both of them are smiling like Cheshire cats. The project manager is very happy that he has a successful project to his name. To bolster this belief, he has a substantial bonus for successful completion in his pocket. Two years later the group have to close the hotel. Occupancy has never exceded 30% and has averaged 18% over the two years. They have made a thumping loss. Was this really a successful project?

So a successful project is not simply one that meets its project aims in terms of cost, time and performance. It must also fulfil the broader purpose of the project. In turnkey projects it is not sufficient that the project is completed within the budget so far as the main contractor and his project manager are concerned. It must also be completed so as to give the planned profit to the contractor. Meeting the project aims in terms of timescale may also involve meeting certain intermediate completion dates. Performance may also involve quantities. For instance, a computer project may involve the supply of 400 terminals. If only half the terminals have actually been supplied by the due dates then this certainly has an impact on the success of the project.

Taking a broad overview of large projects may suggest that our criteria are too narrow. Some projects, even quite unlikely ones, are really in the nature of development projects. They are started with a visionary idea and an outline plan, allied to a determination to create something. The more obvious examples might include certain new aircraft. A less obvious example is the Sydney Opera House, which was formally opened in 1973. This was originally due for completion in 1963. It has cost several times the original estimate of $A7 200 000. Further it is argued that its performance (in terms of numbers of seats, etc) differs from that originally envisaged. Nonetheless, who is to say that the Sydney Opera House project was a failure? The people of Sydney have in the Opera House a magnificent arts centre in a magnificent setting.

Whatever the broader considerations may be, the project manager has a job to do. His success must be judged against the way in which he completes his project on time, to agreed performance standards and within budget. This does not mean that we conceal from ourselves that there will be many changes in the course of the project nor does it overlook the probability that throughout the project he will be trading off cost, performance and time against each other.

Any large project is likely in the course of its life to incur a great deal of detailed change and to involve many problems. This after all is a major reason why a project manager is necessary. When we hear that a large and complex project has gone exactly as planned we are normally suspicious. Projects do go wrong and they do involve problems in consequence. In spite of problems, and quite serious ones at that, a project may still be completed successfully. Why is it that some projects are brought to a successful conclusion and some are not? It was John Churton Collins, who wrote: "The secret of success is known only to those who have not succeeded." There is perhaps more than a grain of truth in this. When you talk to those who have piloted projects through to a successful conclusion they may modestly attribute the success to a number of causes. However, one cause shines through their modesty. Clearly the success should be attributed to a perspicacious and highly efficient project manager.

Taking a hint from John Churton Collins, we believe that a great deal may be learnt about successful project management by studying project failures. The problem here is that few people care to admit failure and even fewer care to publicise their own failure. The laws of libel and slander tend to restrict any inclination of third parties of publicise failure. However, if you care to search for them, there are some accounts in print of projects, that ran into difficulties, even if no one cares to call them failures. They are worth finding and studying. Fortunately, perhaps, some of the worst failures occur in prestige projects. Here there is often quite a lot of publicity in the newspapers and careful reading between the lines may enable you to spot some of the causes of failure.

Large construction projects are notoriously difficult to manage and a great many of them are completed late. In 1968 a working party was set up under the auspices of the National Economic Development Council to inquire into the problems of organisation of large industrial construction sites. Their report "Large Industrial Sites" was published by HMSO in 1970.

In the course of the inquiry a number of contractors engaged in the construction of large industrial projects—such as power stations, chemical plants and oil refineries—were asked to list what they regarded as the most important reasons for delay in completing contracts. The major reasons for delay were given as:

1    Late design changes
2    Late delivery of materials or plant
3    Unexpectedly low labour productivity

Other reasons listed were:

4    Labour disputes
5    Delays in subcontractors' performance
6    Shortages of skilled labour
7    Faulty materials
8    Management problems more difficult than anticipated
9    Faulty workmanship
10   Bad weather
11   Late handover of work
12   Access problems

This inquiry was concerned with delay only and not with failure to meet performance criteria or with overrun costs. Nonetheless, almost inevitably, delay means additional cost. The reasons quoted are, of course, related to very large construction projects. In fact, as we shall see, the list contains a number of items that are common causes of failure whatever field the project lies in.

A project, where plenty of things went wrong was the Sydney Opera House. A great deal has been written about the problems that arose on the project and the reasons for those problems. Two excellent books have been published about the project. *The Sydney Opera House Affair* by M Baume published by Nelson, and *The Other Taj Mahal* by John Yeomans published by Longmans. Both books were written years before the project was completed. Nonetheless, the project had been going for several years when the books were written and there had been plenty of problems. They give a fascinating account of the problems that can and do arise on a really large project.

Sometimes the progress of a project is of such critical importance to the future of a public company that it rates a mention in the annual report and accounts. One of the most open and objective accounts of the problems on a major project we have seen is in the statement of the chairman of Davy-Ashmore Limited with the report and accounts for the year ended 31 March 1969. In this statement he sets out to give a better understanding of what went wrong with the Immingham oil refinery project. It was a large project, worth about £25 million. At the time of the statement it was running one year late and the overrun costs were expected to amount to £12 million. On a single page Sir Douglas Bell gave a bird's eye view of the main problems. Senior managers responsible for large projects are well advised to procure a copy and read it.

Our own experience, and what we have learnt from other projects, suggests to us that the major sources of trouble on projects can be traced to one or more of the following causes:

1    Unclear aim or inadequate definition of requirements
2    Inadequate control of change
3    Poor initial evaluation and plan
4    Inadequate project manager
5    Confusion of responsibility
6    Failure to use available techniques
7    Failure to identify and concentrate on critical items
8    Inadequate information flow
9    Failure of subcontractors
10   Labour troubles: strikes, turnover, morale
11   Faulty equipment, materials and workmanship
12   Accidents or bad weather

Each of these headings will now be considered in turn.

## 17:1 UNCLEAR AIM OR
## INADEQUATE DEFINITION OF REQUIREMENTS

This is in our view the most devastating cause of problems on a project and is indeed a frequent cause of failure. It may sound foolishly simple to say, but if you don't know what you are setting out to do, you are unlikely to do it. The project must be completely defined, right down to the smallest details. The form of the definition will depend upon the industry and the practice within it. In the computer industry, for instance, the baseline document is normally a statement of user requirements. Each party to the project must be fully aware of and underwrite his part of the project definition.

It ought, perhaps, to go without saying that each party involved in the project should understand the same thing from the project definition. Regretably a lack of such a common understanding is frequently a source of project problems and much recrimination. This can be the case particularly where a consortium of several companies of different nationality is formed to execute a project. The need to have this common understanding of the project definition is one that requires careful consideration. The project definition must of course be committed to paper and must be a controlled document. That is to say, every copy of the document must be identical to the others and a system of controlled amendment must be adopted. There is no doubt at all in our minds that a clear, fully documented and agreed project definition is the basis for a successful project.


## 17:2 INADEQUATE CONTROL OF CHANGE

This cause of trouble clearly follows on from the first. It is no use having a clear agreed project definition if the position is allowed to become confused by uncontrolled change in the requirements. We have already referred in considerable detail to the need for change control procedures but we make no excuse for returning to the point. It is absolutely central to the successful management of projects. Anyone who has bought a new house before it is completed knows the irritation and illwill that is generated by changing requirements in the later stages of building. Even apparently minor ones— such as the positioning of power points—become very expensive in the final stages of finishing the house. The problems are worse on a large project.

It is common on a large project to have hundreds or even thousands of project-definition changes proposed. Individually their impact on time-scales, cost and performance may be small but the cumulative effect if not controlled and appreciated may be catastrophic. The impact on all parts of the project must be considered. All the activities in a project mesh together and a change in any one activity is likely to affect others. The effect on the operating and maintenance phase after the project has been completed must also be considered. If a tight and well documented procedure for change is not operated there will be trouble. The procedure must also allow for the user (or customer) who is paying for the project to be told of the impact of the change. The procedure should provide for his formal agreement and instruction to incorporate the change in the project definition. The cost of a good change control procedure may seem high but without it control of a project is lost and costs are bound to increase—probably substantially.

## 17:3  POOR INITIAL EVALUATION AND PLAN

Poor evaluation and planning of any project will clearly lead to problems later on. Much of the evaluation work will have been done on many projects long before a project manager is appointed. Nonetheless, the whole success of this work rests on the soundness of the evaluation on which the decision to go ahead was made. The hotel example quoted at the beginning of this chapter, is an indication of how an otherwise perfectly executed project becomes a failure. The initial evaluation of a project needs to be recorded on paper with all the assumptions on which it is based spelt out and quantified. The project manager must be familiar with the evaluation and the assumptions. In particular he needs to be aware of the sensitivity of the assumptions so that he can take particular care in the areas where a small error in an assumption has a large effect on the project outcome.

To refer to problems arising from poor project planning seems too obvious to say. Yet the need for a sound plan is often ignored or, at best, only lip service is paid to it. When a project is approved and work starts, there is always a tremendous amount to do—time is short; initially available resources maybe inadequate; the key activities appear to be obvious. So some project managers are tempted to "get on with it and let the plan wait." The project gathers momentum and the plan evolves from a chain of decisions. Ideally, almost from day one, the project manager must have a plan. At first it will contain very little detail and will identify only the major activities. However, it should be sufficient for him to construct a first-level network. It can then be broken down and filled in deliberately and as quickly as possible.

An essential aspect of any sound project plan is that the individual parts of the plan have the support of the managers or subcontractors who will carry them out. A sound plan must have a network as part of it. On any project of any size the logical interactions of the various parts of the project can only be realised by the use of a network. Senior management when inspecting an initial project plan should look for simple effects. Has sufficient time been allowed for bringing the necessary resources together? Has time been allowed for user or customer acceptance? Has the critical path through the network been identified and how many of the activities on it are dependent upon external factors? At the beginning of a project the high costs of sound and detailed planning is obvious. What is not so obvious is the mountain of trouble and consequent expense which is being built up if such a plan is not produced.

## 17:4   INADEQUATE PROJECT MANAGER

Perhaps we should have listed this as the prime cause of project problems. One could argue that most other causes stem from a poor project manager. A good one will ensure that there is a firm project definition with a tight well-documented change-control procedure and so on down the list. The whole of Chapter 3 was devoted to the project manager so we will not labour the point. However, senior management must recognise that the success of the project, as with any other activity, depends on the manager. It is worth time and trouble to ensure that you pick good project managers. Further, it is foolish to pay a project manager £5000 a year and expect him to do a £12 000 a year job. The fact that he reports to a line manager, who maybe paid much less, does not matter. The project manager is the key factor in project success. He has to bring a remarkable combination of qualities to his project. He should be suitably rewarded and if possible some part of his reward should be related to project success.

## 17:5   CONFUSION OF RESPONSIBILITY

It is trite to say that everyone concerned with a project should have clearly defined responsibilities. On a complex project, there are many interfaces between the various parties involved and it is necessary that these should be clearly defined. Strangely enough confusion of responsibility occurs quite often where governments are involved. This occurs because while they do not wish to accept responsibility for some aspect of a project, they nonetheless wish to exercise influence on it. This arises both from the cautious approach of the civil servant and also from the politician trying to extend his influence beyond its legitimate limits.

The project manager—or his seniors in the organisation responsible for the execution of the project—is subjected to unfair pressures of all sorts to persuade him to adopt a course that is against his better judgement. Later when his better judgement is vindicated he finds himself carrying the can for a course of action that he was not strong enough to resist.

It is easy for us to write "project responsibilities must be clearly defined." In some projects it is extremely difficult to achieve this. Some of the external influences can be insidious and effective. Nonetheless we must recognise that it is a source of project problems. If complete definition is not possible, then the areas of confusion should at least be recognised and carefully monitored. Care should be taken in particular about the recording and dissemination of decisions.

## 17:6  FAILURE TO USE AVAILABLE TECHNIQUES

Clearly as in any other work, the most effective techniques should be used. Particularly in the project management area itself proven management techniques should be used. Their use in itself will not guarantee success. An intelligent and understanding use of modern project management techniques will help to avoid many problems and to foresee others before it is too late to do something about them. For any large project with a life extending into years the evaluation should make use of discounting techniques such as DCF. We devoted several chapters of our book *Successful Project Management* to the techniques of financial evaluation of projects and refer interested readers to them.

Attempts to control complex projects on the back of an envelope are likely to prove disastrous. If you don't believe it, watch a small local builder trying to use these techniques to erect a couple of houses on an infilling development. For some parts of a project bar charts and graphs will provide a useful tool for judging progress. But to ensure that you get a sound logical lock of all activities some form of networking technique should be used. PERT—programming evaluation and review technique—is the best known and most widely used. If it is used and frequently updated, it certainly helps to highlight the areas that are running into trouble. This may be laborious to do, but computer programs exist to take a lot of the sheer slog out of the work of updating. It is certainly worth putting your network onto a computer if you have more than about 200 activities in it. It is not, of course, necessary to own your own computer. Most commercial computer bureaux offer a PERT service. Again, in assessing project cost, it is necessary to recognise that preparation and updating of a network will cost money. It is money well spent.

It is generally realised that project progress in terms of time must be controlled. However, project progress in terms of cost and resources also need to be controlled and extensions of the PERT techniques help the project manager to do this. A well-prepared and frequently updated network is a great help in deciding what trade-offs between time, cost and performance are worth while. With a computer it is, of course, possible to try out a whole series of alternative courses on your network in a comparatively short space of time.

Techniques are not the be all and end of all successful projects but they can be a great help in forestalling problems. We have mentioned only the more obvious ones but any project manager should find out about and investigate any techniques that could help him.

## 17:7 FAILURE TO IDENTIFY AND CONCENTRATE ON CRITICAL ITEMS

If a project has been properly planned initially and a network for the project produced, then a critical path through the network will have been identified. If the logic that goes into the creation of the network is thoroughly tested then clearly the project manager automatically concentrates his attention on the critical items by focusing on the activities along the critical path. This is an important aid in helping him to decide how to allocate his own time. It is necessary to recognise that projects are dynamic. The network once drawn does not represent a static situation. The critical path, once identified, does not necessarily represent the critical path for all time.

For a complex project with many activities, one would expect to find different activities moving onto or off the critical path at each progress review. This makes it important to have frequent updates of the network and also makes it important not to neglect activities that lie just off the critical path at any instant. Similarly it is wise to watch out for activities, however much float or contingency there is on them, if they start to slip in real time. In other words, if their completion date goes back four weeks at each four weekly review, look out for trouble. We know of one £3.5 million two-year project, which had a £3000 activity with a float of five months. This activity slipped in real time for various reasons until it appeared at last on the critical path, much to the embarrasment of the project manager. Needless to say, more than embarrasment was involved.

## 17:8 INADEQUATE INFORMATION FLOW

Variations against the project plan are inevitable and with a flexible plan a high proportion of variations will be handled without an appreciable impact. However, for this it is essential to have a free and honest flow of information. Some people hug their problems to themselves. An engineering department may have an intractable power supply problem and not mention it because they are sure it is soluble. A manager responsible for the writing and testing of computer programs may consistently over estimate his progress and may even be tempted, if under pressure, to pass on programs for integration as fully tested and proved, when they still require further testing as individual programs. It is in areas such as these, where progress is to a certain extent a matter of judgement, that there is the greatest possibility of problems arising because the information flow is inadequate.

An information system that will warn the project manager promptly of things going wrong is essential to the success of any project. He will only get one if he carefully plans for it. He must set out to establish good relationships with those concerned so that they will not hug their problems close to their chests. As part of this process we believe it is desirable to treat shortfalls in performance against target as unemotionally as possible. When one department falls behind, examine the situation critically but constructively. The emphasis should be on helping to overcome the problems and not on allocating blame. By this we do not mean that weak excuses should be accepted. If necessary, the pressure must be put on but not in such a way as to stop or slow down the flow of accurate and up-to-date information.

## 17:9  FAILURE OF SUBCONTRACTORS

For any project manager, the performance of his subcontractors is a critical factor. In many projects failure of subcontractors to honour their commitments is a frequent cause of late completion. Many of the worst problems on the Immingham Oil Refinery project, to which we refered earlier, arose from the fact that a subcontractor went into liquidation. The whole question of securing a satisfactory performance from subcontractors is beset with difficulties. Again, it is a subject to which we devoted a chapter in *Successful Project Management*.

A project manager tells his subcontractors what he wants from them, and when he wants it. He will also have agreed a price. He normally, however, has no control over how the subcontractor achieves the end result. Even with supervisory or quality staff working closely with the subcontractor it is very difficult to pick up troubles with any degree of confidence. Care also has to be taken not to confuse responsibilities by interfering with the way in which the subcontractor does his work or by bringing unfair influence on his decisions.

Perhaps the most effective way of controlling subcontractors is in the care taken in their selection. In all subcontracting, the best subcontractor is the one that delivers the goods to specification and on time, not necessarily the one that quotes the cheapest price. A minor subcontractor responsible for a few thousand pounds worth of work can hold up a multi-million pound contract for weeks. In a bad case the failure of a subcontractor can cost the project many times the value of the subcontract.

## 17:10  LABOUR TROUBLES: STRIKES, TURNOVER, MORALE

The most publicised type of labour trouble that causes project problems is the strike. A strike among the staff directly involved on a project is the most obvious case. In large construction projects one cause of labour dissatisfaction and of strikes arises from the number of subcontractors on site. Several subcontractors may employ men drawn from the same union but give them different conditions as regards overtime, travelling time and arrangements, subsistance allowance and so on. The result is that whereas the men are happy with the situation in isolation, they resent the unfavourable comparison with the terms given to men in the same union on the same site. Once a problem of this sort develops on a site it can become almost insoluble. An approach adopted by one large firm in such circumstances—on really large £50 million or so projects—is to negotiate conditions direct with each union involved. The terms agreed are then made a mandatory part of each subcontract. This requires a tremendous amount of effort, foresight and negotiating ability but if it can be done the benefits are immense.

In high-technology projects a major problem can be staff turnover. A particularly dangerous stage is towards the end of a project when people feel that they have got all the experience they can from it and wonder where they will go next. A possible approach for the project manager is to overstaff the project in the early days. This makes some wastage comparatively painless. However, it can also be dangerous as the result of underworking people is generally to lower their morale.

Morale is, of course, a major factor in project success as it is in every field of human endeavour. We can not offer you a ready made solution but only remind you that successful projects depend on the people who work on them.

## 17:11  FAULTY EQUIPMENT,
##        MATERIALS AND WORKMANSHIP

This can obviously be a fruitful source of project problems. Once again the main protection against these problems is foresight. The project plan must make adequate allowance for acceptance testing of all components or equipment as it passes from supplier or subcontractor to the project or, even more important, as it passes from one subcontractor to another. So far as is possible, arrangements must be made for quality to be built into the project in all its stages.

Where a complex piece of equipment is being produced by a subcontractor it may be necessary to place a quality inspector in his factory. A project manager is well advised to be very careful about any item of new design which he incorporates in his project. This applies not only to new major items of new design but also to quite minor items like levers or pipes.

## 17:12 ACCIDENTS AND BAD WEATHER

Accidents can happen to the best planned of projects. It is, of course, easy to be wise after the event, but how many of the accidents that occur are genuinely accidents? The word accident is frequently used to describe lack of foresight or planning.

Similarly many project problems are blamed on bad weather. It is true that there are sometimes freak weather conditions and they can have a serious and unexpected effect on a project. However the man who plans to lay concrete in the open in Northern England in February is taking a risk and should recognise that fact rather than blame bad weather when he is held up by frost.

We have reviewed those factors that lead to project success or failure because we believe that they are common to projects in most fields. Attention to these points will contribute a lot to project success. To quote Joseph Addison:

*'Tis not in mortals to command success. But we'll do more, Sempronious, we'll deserve it.*

# Part Seven

# APPENDICES

# *Appendix A*

# Project Case Study

A project case study provides an opportunity to practice some aspects of project management. Doing so, presents a problem as it is difficult to choose a technical subject that will be understood by every reader. We must talk about a technical task because projects in general have a technical content and complexity. However, in this case study we confine ourselves to the "management" of a project without emphasising the technical difficulties that a project manager will face. His ability to deal with these either directly or with assistance must be assumed. In this project, for example, the project manager has in his team an engineering specialist.

We talk in the study of specifications for the equipment, but it would be pointless to detail them. Where the study demands it we have described the part or parts separately in a non-technical manner.

Since the object of a case study is to provide as near practical training as possible, the participants must have in miniature the same conditions as there would be in an actual project:

1   The background knowledge of the project is provided by a description of the companies, people and project state prior to the review that forms the basis of the study. We can, of course, take only a particular point in time; information is flowing all the time in a well-run project and is not saved up for review meetings.

2   Appendix *A* contains the correspondence "in tray"

As a means of self-improvement the following questions should be answered.

## A1   QUESTION 1

1   Decide what actions could be taken to improve the situation described
2   Say why these actions are suggested
3   Say whether additional information is necessary or should be sought at this time by the project manager
4   Comment on any aspect of the project arrangements which you feel is unsatisfactory

## A2   QUESTION 2

Prepare a project plan, assuming nothing can or will be done about any of the delays mentioned throughout the study. In this connection take account of the latest information of each aspect:

1   Say when the first Post Office line ought to be available
2   What is the earliest date for completion of the operation trials

## A3   PROJECT IN BRIEF

The project under examination is the implementation of a computer system for Allied Warehouses in the customer's new building. It includes the special development of a terminal for each of the nine remote depots of the customer and provides a stock and order control system. The project involves several subcontractors. The main contractor is the computer manufacturer, Martin International. Private telephone lines to be provided by the Post Office will link each depot terminal to the computer headquarters in London.

A complete definition of the task has been agreed with the customer and a detailed requirement specification also agreed for the terminal. This will be a standard device bought from a manufacturer in Germany, but fairly extensively modified by the main contractor. The customer will start to use the system with the depot nearest to the new building. Three other depots will be connected to the system three months after satisfactory tests and operation of the first. The remaining five depots will have their terminals installed within the following six months.

The new building will not only house the computer, but provide office accommodation for the computer operators, programmers and planning staff. The computer will be used for payroll and ultimately management information services as well as the stock and order control work.

## A4   CONTRACT

The key points in the contract are certain dates and details of penalties, as follows:

*By customer*
1   The computer room will be ready for the computer by week 84 (i.e. eighty-four weeks after contract signing).
2   Penalties are payable to the computer manufacture if the room is later than five weeks after week 84 at the rate of £2000 a week for each week of delay.
3   The customer has said he will use all reasonable endeavours in respect of the programming he has to do so that the contractor will not be delayed with the further phases of work. The aims are to complete program writing at week 66 with final program trials for eighteen weeks after the computer to terminal link testing. This latter will take four weeks. There will be a period of eight weeks operational trials after the final program trials.

*By supplier.*   The computer will be installed within three weeks after the computer room is ready (expected at 84) but the supplier is not obliged to complete the installation until the end of week 87. After this penalties would be payable at £2000 a week.

*Main contractor's plans*
1   Apart from times in the contract Martin International has planned to build the computer by week 65 and test it for four weeks in the factory. After this a system test, using the first terminal, will be run for twelve weeks also in the factory.
2   The terminal which arrived in week 50, has twenty weeks allowed for modifications, new covers and testing before it joins the computer for the system tests.
3   Special cables are required for the terminal sites, these are long-delivery (seventy weeks) and the installation of them will take five weeks.
4   Terminals two to four are planned to arrive at week 72 and will require ten weeks' modification and test work before sending to the next three sites.

## A5   COMPANIES

1   The main contractor is a medium-sized computer manufacturer, Martin International, of some fifteen years' standing. It has approximately 20 000

employees, a headquarters where engineering, software and marketing activities are carried out and three factories. We shall know the factories as M1, M2 and M3 and the engineering department as MLAB. The project management is operated from the marketing organisation, as shown on the management chart. (The Chart (Figure A1) is only completed sufficiently to show the case study interrelationships.)

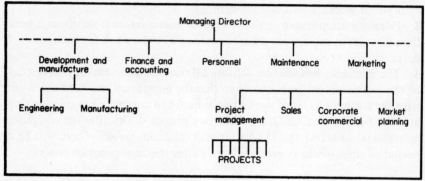

**Figure A1 ORGANISATION CHART**

2 Special Plated Products Limited is a small company supplying memory stores of advanced design to Martin International. It is an efficient unit and the computer manufacturer has dealt with the company for several years. Relationships are good. Special Plated Products has two factories about five miles from each other. The main factory is in Needham Newtown.

3 Müller & Hart, Düsseldorf. This German company concentrates on specialised terminals for stock and order control. The chosen terminal is not yet in production, but a prototype had been seen at the start and the first preproduction unit has arrived at Martin International.

4 Pack Power Limited is a local subcontractor that has supplied power supplies to Martin International for about three years.

5 Cableways Contracts Limited is a company chosen to carry out cabling in the depots for the terminals. The main contractor has not used this company before, but the terminal manufacturer, Müller & Hart, have had some connections with it on a previous occasion and suggested that the company might be suitable for this project.

6 Sheet Metal Limited is a local subcontractor that Martin International use when their own sheet metal shop is fully loaded. They are moderately reliable and are used because they are local and reasonably priced.

7 Allied Warehouses is the customer and its business is concerned with supplying the retail hardware trade.

## A6   PEOPLE

*Martin International*
1   David Litton, the project manager, is forty-three and in the last seven years has had experience in the engineering, manufacturing and corporate planning areas of the company. He has been in the project management organisation for two and a half years.
2   John Card (thirty-five) is a project leader in the engineering division. He has been allocated to work on this project, temporarily reporting to David Litton.
3   Charles Curren (forty-nine) is the quality assurance manager in factory M1. He has been with the company for five years, after spending much of his career in aeronautical electronic engineering and testing department of the Civil Service.
4   Richard Knock (thirty-eight) is Deputy Manager of M1 factory, has been in works management for the last ten years.
5   Burt Temquick (forty) is a member of the corporate commercial organisation and will carry out all contract negotiations and arrangements for David Litton.
6   Alfred Circuit is manager of the engineering division.
7   Michael South (thirty-three) is the sales executive responsible for selling to Allied Warhouses and works closely with David Litton. He is also responsible for about six other potential customers in his area.

*Customer*
1   Tony Clark aged thirty-seven is the project manager
2   David Anscombe—systems manager reporting to Tony Clark
3   Mr Whitelow—communications engineer for the customer

RREVIEW DATE—60 WEEKS FROM START—MONDAY WEEK 61

The project manager, David Litton, holds a project meeting every Monday on all aspects of his project. He will also meet the customer on the coming Wednesday at a regular two-weekly progress meeting. The information received comes from various sources, sometimes direct from the subcontractors, sometimes via his own company factories or engineering groups.
    In attendance on this occasion are John Card, Charles Curran, Richard Knock and Burt Temquick. A standard agenda is used each week and covers the major aspects of:

1   Engineering
2   Manufacturing and purchasing

3   Timescales
4   Costs
5   Other matters

The minutes of the meetings are always as brief as possible and cover only items of importance after a full discussion on all aspects of the project.

*Engineering* (John Card).   The project leader confirmed the information he had given the project manager on the previous Friday afternoon. A basic fault in the terminal key board had been unearthed by the M1 engineering department and urgent talks were being held with Müller & Hart. The latter admitted that symptoms of the fault had also shown up intermittently in their own models. They were working hard on the trouble but did not expect a modification kit to be available for at least five weeks. The engineering project leader said that when the modification kits became available they would need two extra weeks in the program for installation and retesting. He said that the subcontractor would not budge from the estimated times he had given.

M1 engineering also reported that their own modifications to the terminal including its installation into another cabinet, new electronics and an additional lamp display board, were running into cost trouble. The original estimate for the work was £9000 development charges including production introduction costs. The development costs were now estimated to rise to £12 000.

*Manufacturing* (Richard Knock)
1   Production costs (including production introduction) for the terminal were now estimated at £650 not £500. (The bought-in value of the terminal was £1500 and the sales price offer to the customer was £4000.)
2   The effect of the letter from Special Plated Products concerning the memory stores would cause a delay in the computer build completion by eight weeks. There was no alternative arrangement. (A letter from Special Plated Products to the Corporate Commercial Organisation and copied to the project manager was received that morning.) (See "in tray," page 183.)

*Timescales* (David Litton)
1   The installation of the completed first system would be contingent anyway on the computer room preparation by the customer which Litton had heard was running ten weeks late. The effects of the other recent information was still to be studied and the computer room delay would have to be

checked formally with the customer at the Wednesday meeting.
**2** Litton said that he had noticed two omissions from the project work plan.
**a** Installation of the terminal after dispatch—taking up one week.
**b** The dismantling and dispatch of the computer and terminal to their respective sites would take three weeks, each immediately after computer terminal system tests.

*Costs and commercial items* (Burt Temquick)
**1** He reported that there was a strong rumour that Cableways Contracts was very close to collapse.
**2** Müller & Hart wanted to charge £200 for each modification kit. It stated it was losing money on the terminals because of the special price it had quoted. (It was agreed David Litton and Burt Temquick would discuss this later.)

*Other matters*
**1** Charles Curran reported that the quality of work by Sheet Metal Limited, that was making the new cabinets for the terminals, was not very good and two had already been rejected. If number 3 attempt was not right, then delays might arise on the project. There were still a couple of weeks before this became critical. Richard Knock said that the sheet metal shop was still fully loaded for the next fifteen months.
**2** Charles Curran also reported that Pack Power Limited was not doing well on the new power supplies for the terminals. No formal rejection had yet taken place, but he was suspicious of the ultimate reliability and was having some more tests carried out.

MONDAY LUNCH TIME—WEEK 61

The project manager sat next to the group accountant who told him that he had heard earlier that morning that Cableways Contracts might be in serious financial trouble. The accountant suggested that the project manager should take this into consideration on his project. (Cableways were carrying out cabling in the depots where the terminals were to be situated.) Special cable was needed and was on long delivery. The order for the cable required delivery to be made to Cableways Contracts.

MONDAY AFTERNOON—WEEK 61

Litton gets together with John Card, Alfred Circuit (Card's manager), and Richard Knock, for a further discussion on the timescale extensions stated in the telex from Müller & Hart, and due to the memory stores delay from Special Plated Products.

Müller & Hart told Litton, when he phoned them, that the five-week delay could be shortened to three weeks by night working, if Martin International would help with the cost. They would telex this cost on Tuesday morning. Litton said he would have to consider this, but in any case felt strongly that Martin International should not have to pay. The fault was clearly the responsibility of Müller & Hart.

The meeting then discussed the memory stores. Temquick repeated the same as yesterday—i.e. that the computer would be late by eight weeks.

Litton then said he had had a quick word with marketing about a reallocation of priorities on the stores. Apparently, something could be done by rearranging customer priorities and the likely result would be a two-week saving. However, this would be at the expense of another of the sales Michael South was working on. Litton would have to talk to South about it.

TUESDAY MORNING—WEEK 61 (see "in tray")

MEETING WITH THE CUSTOMER—WEDNESDAY WEEK 61

Also present at the meeting was the sales executive from Martin International (Michael South), with Mr Anscombe, the customer's computer systems manager, and Mr Whitelow, the customer's communications engineer. The Wednesday meeting had a substantially fixed agenda, consisting of the following items:

1   Building
2   Computer and terminal hardware
3   Customer planning and programming
4   Implementation timescale
5   Project costs

Mr Clark reported that the building seemed to be running about fourteen weeks late. His company's works department was still holding intense conversations with the building contractor to find ways to shorten this fourteen weeks delay. He would keep Martin International informed and hoped by the weekend to make a definite statement.

David Litton then reported on progress. The development work on the terminal was running several weeks late, and there was difficulty about the computer date because of the delay to the memory stores. He was still assessing the exact effect, and he would report upon this within a few days.

## IN TRAY

Special Plated Products Limited
Wireways Road
Needham Newtown
Wessex

Thursday (week 60)

Mr E Temquick,
Corporate Commercial Organisation
Martin International
Software Lane
Bintown

Dear Mr Temquick,

I am sorry to inform you that there will be a delay in the delivery to you of the plated quartz memory stores you have on order for your computers. Unfortunately, a fire in our plating plant badly damaged the chemical cleaning section.

Limited alternative production will be carried out at our other factory in Leavetown, but at the best we cannot resume delivery to you for another three weeks. At that time instead of ten stores a weeks, we shall only be able to supply three a week for about five weeks. After this time we can increase to seven a week for four weeks. In twelve weeks from now we hope to resume production at Needham at the full rate.

I can only say how sorry I am at this misfortune for both of us. I will keep in close touch with you over the coming weeks, and you may be sure of our urgent efforts on your behalf.

Yours sincerely,

*Y Oluck*
(production manager)

## IN TRAY

From:                                      To:
Corporate Commercial Organisation          Mr R Knock
Friday Week 60                             Deputy Manager
                                           Factory M1

Subject :   Plated stores from special plated products

I have investigated the effects as far as we are concerned in customer allocation and confirm our telephone conversation on the subject. I understand
that the effect on Allied Warehouses is an eight-week delay.

*A E Temquick*

## IN TRAY

Memo From Charles Curran to David Litton           Thursday (week 61)
(c. c. Mr J Card)

Subject :   Power supplies—allied warehouses project

I have now had the results of tests on the power supplies that will be fitted
in terminals 2 to 9. The control circuit is defective in that under certain
conditions of load it causes the output voltage to be outside of limits. I
have contacted Pack Power but, unfortunately, the close limits called for
are not going to be easy in a redesign. I anticipate several weeks' delay,
possibly up to six, before this is cured. I am looking at alternatives, but am
not hopeful of the result. Could John Card check the first terminal and the
power supply specification to see if there is latitude for a respecification of
voltage limits?

*Charles Curran*
(manager OA)

In looking at the overall implementation timescale Clark stressed that
Martin International must try to retrieve the delays in the program due to
the terminal as he might yet save time on the building.

With regard to programming Clark said this was on time and should be ready as planned. In looking at project costs Clark said that a further examination of the effects of hardware breakdown when the system was in service led him to believe that the terminals should be duplicated in each site and that the cost of this was considered worth while. Michael South promised to quote for this after discussions with Litton on any engineering and system problems.

THURSDAY MORNING—WEEK 61

Litton sees South about the additional terminals and they agree that the additional switching required is standard and presents no technical problems. However, the equipment has to be fitted before the first terminal is tested with the computer. The fitting and wiring will take one week but can be done before the terminal arrives. There is no delivery problem.

Litton also dealt with further reports on progress which had been received that morning. A telex had been received from Müller & Hart stating that the cost of bringing the delay on the terminal modification down to three weeks would be £1000.

FRIDAY AFTERNOON—WEEK 61

Litton receives a telephone call from Clark. Clark tells him that a letter is in the post stating that the building will now definitely be late but only by eight weeks, unless there are completely unforeseen and severe setbacks. He (Clark) had got his works department to get another opinion on progress and a new detailed plan had been drawn up.

Litton did not commit himself at that stage to Clark, about the computer and terminal delays but promised to ring him back on Monday.

## A7   CASE STUDY COMMENTARY

The case study situation described above, provides a snapshot of the situation that might face David Litton, the project manager in week 61 of the project.

Inevitably, we have simplified the situation. The project manager in real life is carrying in his head a vast amount of background knowledge of the industry and the company for which he works. He also has over a year's experience of concentrating on the problems of this particular project.

We would emphasise at this stage that there is no one right way of dealing with the situation. We have taken a look at a particular time in the life of the project. The situation, seen in weeks 60 and 61, is changing rapidly, No doubt there will be many more changes before project completion. We give

below the points that we believe you should have considered in reaching
your answers.

## A:8   QUESTION 1

We believe that action should be taken to improve the situation under the
following headings.

**1** Immediate action should be taken to prevent the cable being delivered to
Cableway Contracts. If the cable is delivered to them and they go bankrupt,
Martin International will find it difficult, if not impossible to recover the
cable. Even if they did succeed in recovering it there would inevitably be
delay to the project. The cable manufacturers should be immediately
instructed to deliver the cable to Martin International. This should be done
in writing and an acknowledgement obtained. To make quite sure that
nothing goes wrong, knowing that the lead time for cable is seventy weeks,
Litton should check the delivery instructions again with the cable manufacturer before the delivery date.

**2** The whole contract position *vis à vis* Cableway Contracts must be reviewed to see what action can be taken to safeguard Martin International.
In parallel, action should be taken to identify an alternative subcontractor,
and to enter into preliminary negotiations with him about price and dates.
How far you can go will depend, of course, on what you find in the examination of the Cableway Contracts contract and also on whether they do in fact
go into liquidation.

**3** Litton should investigate the possibility of continuing work on the terminals, using the present power pack as an interim measure while work goes on
to produce the necessary improved power packs. Litton will have to ask a
number of questions about cost, practicability of change from one power
pack to the other at a later stage and effect on timescales.

**4** Litton should press Special Plated Products to work overtime to try to
reduce the delay to the memory stores. If the only way to persuade Special
Plated Products to do so is to pay them extra to cover the cost of overtime,
he should be prepared to do so.

**5** Litton should instruct Müller and Hart to take all necessary action to
improve delivery of the terminals. He should lean on them very heavily—
if necessarily flying out to call on their managing director. The fact that
they quoted a very tight "special" price is their own affair. The effect of their
delinquency on future business should be stressed. Litton should avoid any
committment to pay for the necessary extra effort. The full implications of
the modification should also be investigated.

**6** Litton should arrange for an inspector to visit Sheet Metal Limited to

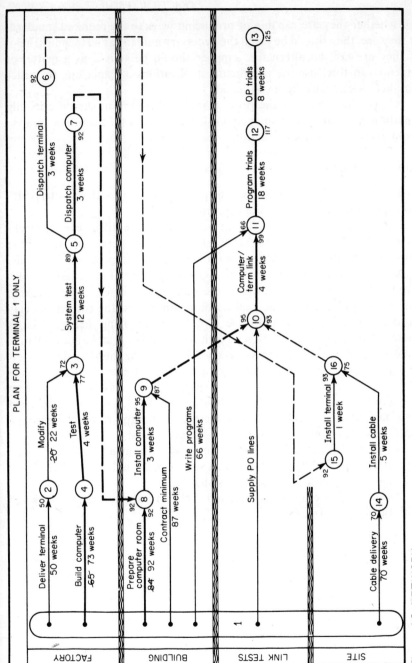

Figure A2 NETWORK

187

see whether they are capable of producing work to the required standard. If they are, they should be given the necessary guidance and technical help. If they are not, an alternative supplier should be sought as a matter of urgency. In this case the contractual implications of cancelling the order on Sheet Metal must be investigated.

7   Given the state that the project has reached Litton should critically question his own performance and ask himself how far the problems arise from his actions or lack of action.

## A:9   QUESTION 2

The network in Figure 42 shows one possible solution with the interpretations possible from reading the case study.

Since the review is taking place at week 61 there are still nine or ten weeks to go before the end of the twenty-week modification period allowed for the terminal and it has been stated that the effect of the problems being discussed with M & H will be an extra two weeks on top of this twenty weeks. From this, apart from all normal project management actions being taken, one might presume that no real account other than the two-week delay need be taken of the actual M & H delay in supplying their mod-kit as there will be time to fit it. The net result of this will be that the accumulative time at event 3 will be seventy-seven weeks assuming the store delay is left at eight weeks. This gives carry forward figures at event 5 of eighty-nine weeks and at event 7 of ninety-two weeks, and so on, as can be seen from the network. The critical path runs from event 13 at 125 weeks total project time back through 12,11,10,9 and 8. Here the critical path branches through 7,5,3,4 and 1, one way and direct to 1 the other way.

The date on which the Post Office line ought to be available should not be later than week 95 but it is certain that some work could be done before this date in order to ensure a smooth installation.

The earliest date for the completion of the operational trials is week 125 with the assumptions made.

# Appendix B

# Network Problem
## —and Answer

An engineering company has to bring down the unit price of a long-run product and decides to carry out a study, with the help of a specialist consultant, into the possibility of purchasing a new automatic machine. This is a very sophisticated machine, mainly computer operated and is on long delivery. The study period is expected to take sixteen weeks, during which time a complete examination of all the relevant factors will be made including returns on capital, machine delivery time and associated timetable of work. The company were also already embarked on a study for a new factory in which the computer would be housed, among other things. The computer would not only be capable of operating the new machine but of doing a number of useful housekeeping jobs for the company including payroll, personnel files, some management information services and some production control generally.

The study in the end turned out to be easier than expected and took twelve weeks instead of sixteen. The delivery of the machine was ascertained to be ninety weeks and an order was placed immediately at the end of the study. All other items mentioned in this network example start from the end of the study period.

Before the machine goes into service training must be given to a number of operators. Six weeks is allowed for this but prior to training suitable people have to found. This was not thought to be easy because of the very specialised work, and to give time to find the best candidates a fifteen-week recruitment period is planned.

As the machine is to be mainly computer operated a suite of programs has to be specially written although some standard items will be available from the machine supplier. A period of fifteen weeks after the study is allowed to enable recruitment, after this the programs will take sixty-five weeks to write. The finished programs will be tested on the computer for twelve weeks to ensure they are fully effective short of testing them with the machine itself under control.

The factory construction will be in two phases, the first, enabling the computer room to be built in it will take thirty weeks. The computer room itself will take a further eight weeks to finish. This will then be ready for air conditioning to be installed over the next twelve weeks.

The computer delivery and installation is estimated by the computer supplier to be eighty weeks from order and the order was placed at the end of the study. However, delivery will not be made until the air conditioning is complete. The installation will take three weeks. When the computer is installed hardware acceptance tests will be carried out for four weeks. These tests will be the normal quality control tests of the computer supplier.

Phase two of the building program will be completed thirty-five weeks after phase one. It will allow the preparation of the site for the machine. The initial work for this will be getting ready for concreting. Two weeks are allowed. The concreting itself has to be done in a special manner and will take one week. This week also includes the setting out of appropriate fixings for the machine. The concrete will form a very strong and deep concrete raft. This raft will take eight weeks to fully set before it is ready to receive the machine. The installation of the machine will be carried out over a four-week period. Although the machine will not produce any suitable output before it has bedded down on the concrete for a further three weeks after installation it can be used for tests with the computer to finally prove the programs. This is planned immediately after installation for two weeks.

The machine will be subjected to acceptance tests after the final settling in time of two weeks, but special materials have to be obtained to do this. The order for these was placed immediately after the study but the delivery was long, eighty weeks.

As the project progressed along its path it became obvious, as it often does in a project, that certain changes would have to be made to the project plan. The items were as follows. The computer supplier now said that delivery could be earlier and indeed they would appreciate earlier acceptance because of the end of their financial year. The net result was a delivery promise twelve weeks earlier than before. The engineering company agreed to this as they had no reason to suppose that they could not ac-

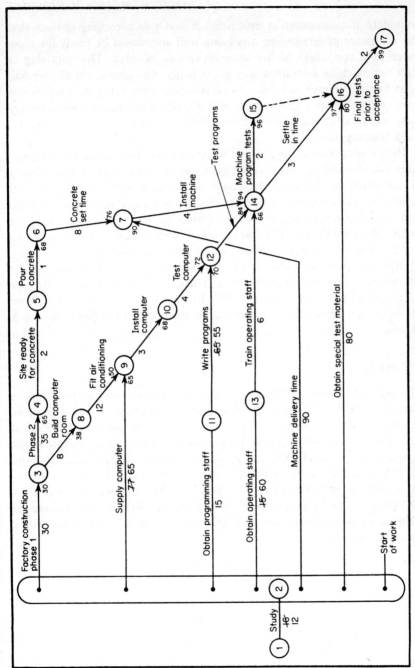

Figure BI   NETWORK PROBLEM   All times are in weeks totalled from event 2

191

comodate the computer at that time. It was also becoming obvious that the computer programming was going well and would be ready for computer tests ten weeks earlier than previously planned. The obtaining of staff for machine operation was going badly; no suitable candidates had been found although new lines of recruitment were being pursued. It was now admitted that recruitment could not be complete until week 60, i.e. sixty weeks after study completion. There was still no change to the six-week training plan.

The project manager appointed for the project by the engineering company was also finding out other things that were of vital interest. The delivery of the machine, for example, could be brought forward if this was of benefit but extra costs would be payable. He knew that the machine operation would save the company £2000 a week but that the earlier delivery of the machine would cost £10 000 for a ten-week saving in time. Ten weeks was the best saving that could be made by the machine supplier.

Draw the planning network for the project as outlined showing all the changes and state whether the project manager would be likely to take advantage of the earlier delivery offer by the machine supplier. Calculate the total time before the machine was producing after the end of the study period.

## ANSWER

The network shown in Figure B1 has taken into account all the changes mentioned in the text except the final decision on whether it is worth while getting an earlier delivery of the machine. It can be seen that the critical path does in fact run up through the machine delivery time as one might expect. The cost is £10 000 for ten weeks. Ten weeks off would bring the accumulative time at event 14 from event 7 down to 84 the same as the accumulation from event 12 to 14 which was the next critical path. Thus ten weeks could be saved off the whole job and if the saving was indeed £2000 a week as stated then £10 000 would be saved by recommending the earlier delivery.

# Bibliography

## BOOKS

BAUMGARTNER, J S, *Project Manager*, Irwin (USA), 1963

BAUME, M, *The Sydney Opera House Affair*, Nelson, 1967

BRECH, E F L (editor) *Construction Management in Principle and Practise*, Longmans, 1971.

BRICHTA, A M, and SHARP, P E M, *From Project to Production*, Pergamon Press, 1970

CLELAND, D I, and KING, W R, *Systems Analysis and Project Management*, McGraw-Hill, 1968

HACKNEY, J M, *Control and Management of Capital Projects*, Wiley, 1965

LOCK, D, *Project Management*, Gower Press, 1968

LOWE, C W, *Critical Path Analysis by Bar Chart*, Business Books, 1969

MODER, J J, and PHILLIPS, C R, *Project Management with CPM and PERT*, Chapman & Hall, 1964

PATON, T A L, (Chairman) *Large Industrial Sites*, Report of a National Economic Development Office working party, HMSO, 1970

ROLT, L T C, *Isambard Kingdom Brunel*, Penguin, 1970

SILVERMAN, M, *The Technical Program Manager's Guide to Survival*, Wiley, 1967

STEINER, G A, and RYAN, W G, *Industrial Project Management*, MacMillan (USA), 1968

TAYLOR, W J, and WATLING, T F, *Successful Project Management*, Business Books, 1972

TAYLOR, W J, and WATLING, T F, *The Basic Arts of Management*, Business Books, 1972

WOODGATE, H S, *Planning by Network*, Business Books, 1967

YEOMANS, J, *The Other Taj Mahal*, Longmans, 1968

ZUCKERMAN, SIR S, (Chairman) *Technological Innovation in Britain*, Report of the Central Advisory Council of Science & Technology, HMSO, 1968

ARTICLES

AVOTS, I, "Why does Project Management Fail?" *California Management Review*, Fall 1969, volume XII, number 1.

AVOTS, I, "Making Project Management Work," *Datamation*, January 1973

BERGER, M, "If Noah Built the Ark Today," *Management Review*, July 1969

BLOCK, E B, "Accomplishment/Cost: Better Project Control," *Harvard Business Review*, May–June 1971

BLYTH, A H, "Design of Incentive Contracts, Basic Principles," *The Aeronautical Journal*, volume 73, number 698, February 1969

BROOKS, P W, "Management and Marketing in Large Enterprises," *The Aeronautical Journal*, volume 74, number 720, December, 1970

CLELAND, D I, "Why Project Management?" *Business Horizons*, Winter 1964

CLELAND, D I, "Understanding Project Authority," *Business Horizons*, Spring 1967

EYIONS, D A, "The Turnkey Concept," *Data Processing*, May–June 1969

GADDIS, P O, "The Project Manager," *Harvard Business Review*, May–June 1959

HERTZ, D B, "Risk Analysis in Capital Investment," *Harvard Business Review*, January–February 1964

HILL, N D, and WATLING, T F, "The Impact of LACES," Computer Communications: Impacts & Implications, The procedings of the First International Conference on Computer Communication, Washington, October 1972

HOLLANDER, G L, and TILLEY, E A, "Optimise your Project Management," *Computer Decisions*, November 1972

HOWELL, R A, "Multi Project Control," *Harvard Business Review*, March–April 1968

JONASON, P, "Project Management Swedish Style," *Harvard Business Review*, November–December 1971

JOYNER, K J, "Business Engineering Evolution of the Project Manager," *Civil Engineering*, May 1972

MIDDLETON, C J, "How to set up a Project Organisation," *Harvard Business Review*, March–April 1967

SHAIN, M, "Acceptance Trials for a Real Time System," *The Computer Journal*, volume 15, number 4

SPIER, G L E, "Project Assessment," *The Director*, October 1966

TAYLOR, W J, and WATLING, T F, "Successful Project Control," *Accountancy* December 1972

THOMPSON, P A, "Cost of Indecision," *The Consulting Engineer*, March 1970

TOMLIN, R, "A PERT Plan for Computer Installation," *European Business*, April 1970

WALKER, D, "The Influences of Incentive Provisions on Project Management," *The Aeronautical Journal*, volume 74, number 720, December 1970

WEARNE, S H, "Project and Product Responsibilities in Industry," *Management Decision*, Winter 1970

WEARNE, S H, "The Making of a Project Manager," *The Guardian*, 3 June 1971

WOOD, K, "The Project System," *The Guardian*, 6 November 1970


OTHER SOURCES

DAVY-ASHMORE, *Annual Report & Accounts*, 1969

"The management of consortia for major contracts," proceedings of a symposium, British Institute of Management, 1970


RELATED BIBLIOGRAPHIES

"A shorter list of books and papers on engineering project management," prepared by S H Wearne, The University of Manchester Institute of Science and Technology, 3rd edition, January 1971

*Project Planning*, British Institute of Management, September 1970

# Index